What You Can Do About Do About STRESS AND ANXIETY

What You Can Do About STRESS AND ANXIETY

Enslow Publishing
101 W. 23rd Street
Suite 240
New York, NY 10011
USA

enslow.com

**Jennifer Way and
Sara Van Duyne**

Published in 2016 by Enslow Publishing, LLC
101 W. 23rd Street, Suite 240, New York, NY 10011

Library of Congress Cataloging-in-Publication Data
Way, Jennifer.
 What you can do about stress and anxiety / Jennifer Way and Sara Van Duyne.
   pages cm. — (Contemporary diseases and disorders)
 Audience: Age 12-up.
 Audience: Grade 7 to 8.
 Summary: "Describes the conditions associated with stress and anxiety, including symptoms, the latest research, and treatment options"— Provided by publisher.
 Includes bibliographical references and index.
 ISBN 978-0-7660-7042-4
 1. Stress management—Juvenile literature. 2. Anxiety—Juvenile literature. 3. Obsessive compulsive disorder—Juvenile literature. 4. Phobias—Juvenile literature. I. Van Duyne, Sara. II. Title.
 RA785.W39 2016
 616.85'227—dc23
                        2015015553

Printed in the United States of America

To Our Readers: We have done our best to make sure all Web site addresses in this book were active and appropriate when we went to press. However, the author and the publisher have no control over and assume no liability for the material available on those Web sites or on any Web sites they may link to. Any comments or suggestions can be sent by e-mail to customerservice@enslow.com.

Portions of this book originally appeared in the book *Stress and Anxiety-Related Disorders*.

Disclaimer: For many of the images in this book, the people photographed are models. The depictions do not imply actual situations or events.

Photo Credits: © AP Images, pp. 25, 59, 81; Boston Globe/Boston Globe/Getty Images, p. 83; Brian C. Weed/Shutterstock.com, p. 76; CREATISTA/Shutterstock.com, p. 41; Designua/Shutterstock.com, p. 15; DreamBig/Shutterstock.com, p. 52; Enslow Publishing, LLC, p. 13; Goodluz/Shutterstock.com, p. 73; hxdbzxy/Shutterstock.com, p. 10; © iStockphoto.com/4774344sean, p. 80; KUCO/Shutterstock.com, p. 49; margo_black/Shutterstock.com, p. 3; Marwan Ibrahim/AFP/Getty Images, p. 57; maxim ibragimov/Shutterstock.com, p. 23; New York Times Co./Archive Photos/Getty Images, p. 65; Paul Matthew Photography/Shutterstock.com, p. 71; Photographee.eu/Shutterstock.com, p. 78; pjhpix/Shutterstock.com, p. 46; Science & Society Picture Library/SSPL/Getty Images, p. 19; StockStudio/Shutterstock.com, p. 88; The Washington Post/The Washington Post/Getty Images, p. 61; Triff/Shutterstock.com, p. 90; ullstein bild/ullstein bild/Getty Images, p. 21; val lawless/Shutterstock.com, p. 45; Viacheslav Nikolaenko/Shutterstock.com, p. 67; Volt Collection/Shutterstock.com, p. 35; wavebreakmedia/Shutterstock.com, p. 31.

Cover Credit: margo_black/Shutterstock.com (crying girl).

CONTENTS

Stress and Anxiety Disorders at a Glance 6

1 Interfering With Life 8

2 Anxiety Disorders in History 17

3 What Is OCD? 28

4 What Are Phobias? 38

5 Panic Attacks and Panic Disorder 48

6 What Is PTSD? 56

7 Generalized Anxiety Disorder 63

8 Treating Anxiety 70

9 Anxiety, Society, and Research 85

Top 10 Questions and Answers 92

Timeline of Stress and Anxiety 95

Chapter Notes 96

Glossary 104

For More Information 107

Further Reading 109

Index 110

STRESS AND ANXIETY DISORDERS AT A GLANCE

WHAT ARE THEY?

Anxiety-related disorders are the most common type of mental illness. While everyone experiences nervous, uneasy feelings of anxiety from time to time, a person with an anxiety disorder experiences a level of anxiety that affects his or her daily life. There are several types of stress and anxiety-related disorders, and each has its own range of symptoms.

WHO GETS THEM?

People from every kind of background can develop an anxiety disorder. People of all ages—kids, teenagers, young adults, and older adults—may have an anxiety disorder, too. That said, some anxiety disorders are more common in people from certain background or age groups, and some anxiety disorders are more common in women than in men.

WHY DO PEOPLE GET THEM?

The main contributing factors to developing anxiety disorders are thought to be genetics and stress. Some people inherit genes from their parents that make them susceptible. (Genes are short sections of DNA that carry chemical instructions that determine an organism's traits.) If these people suffer stressful life experiences, they are more likely to develop an anxiety disorder. In addition, social modeling, in which behavior is learned through observing others, may play a part. With some anxiety disorders, biological factors, such as bacteria or toxins, may be contributing causes.

WHAT ARE THE SYMPTOMS?

The symptoms of anxiety disorders vary widely. For example, a person with an obsessive-compulsive disorder (OCD) may wash his or her hands many times a day. A person who gets panic attacks unexpectedly experiences feelings of extreme dread along with physical symptoms that mimic a heart attack. In post-traumatic stress disorder (PTSD), the person cannot help reliving past terrors and is emotionally numb and on edge.

HOW ARE THEY TREATED?

The main treatments for anxiety disorders are medications and a type of psychotherapy called cognitive-behavioral therapy (CBT). In CBT, the patient and therapist work together to change behaviors and negative patterns of thought.

CAN THEY BE PREVENTED?

So far, not a great deal is understood about preventing anxiety disorders. It is known, though, that ongoing high levels of stress put people at risk. As awareness of anxiety disorders becomes more widespread, they will be recognized early on. Early intervention helps to control them.

INTERFERING WITH LIFE

David literally spent two years living in his bathroom. He didn't come out for any holidays or his birthday. He stayed in there by himself, and months went by when he couldn't bring himself to open the door even a crack. His parents had to bring him flat foods that could be slid under the door. During those two years, David sometimes showered for twelve hours at a time. He scrubbed the bathroom floor on his hands and knees. He agonized over the possibility that he might have passed on germs to his parents as they passed food under the door and pleaded with them to wash their clothes and shower.

David has an anxiety disorder. This is a condition of severe anxiety that seriously interferes with his life. The kind of anxiety disorder that he has is obsessive-compulsive disorder (OCD). One of the symptoms of OCD is obsessions, or unwanted, persistent thoughts that come into the mind repeatedly. David's persistent thoughts are of germs and contamination. Another symptom of OCD is compulsions, or actions the person feels forced to perform. David's compulsions are washing and cleaning. Compulsions are carried out to lessen the anxiety caused by the obsessions.

David knew that what he was doing made no sense, but even so he could not stop. At twenty-seven, he felt he had not accomplished anything in life. And he had high goals for himself. He had been a fine philosophy student in college. He aspired to earn a doctorate degree and become a professor. When his anxiety would let up, David made good use of his time. He read from a tall stack of books in the corner—classics and nonfiction. And he played chess on parallel boards with his father. Still, it is a long journey from living in a bathroom to being a philosophy professor.

David knew that what he was doing made no sense, but even so he could not stop.

The first signs of David's illness had come when he was a child. When he was eight, he began washing his hands for about fifteen minutes at a time. Slowly, over the years, his illness progressed. If he had been treated early on, with treatments that are available today, he likely would not have ended up living in a bathroom.

Eventually David's story was told on the CBS news show *48 Hours*.[1] The editors of that show put David in touch with Dr. Michael Jenike, a psychiatrist in the Boston area who specializes in treating people with OCD. Dr. Jenike traveled eight hundred miles to David's home. He began treating David with medication and very gradual exposure to the things he fears. With treatment, David managed to emerge from the bathroom for longer and longer periods. He was eventually even able to take trips away from home. Although David will probably never be completely cured, he should be able to maintain good control over his symptoms. The chances are excellent that he will be able to realize many of his goals.

An obsession with germs may be accompanied by a compulsion to repeatedly wash hands or take a shower.

NORMAL ANXIETY VS. ANXIETY DISORDER

Anxiety is an uneasy feeling, usually about something in the future. All human beings experience anxiety at times. It is normal. In fact, it is vital to survival. If we felt too safe, we might not survive. As one joke goes, "Anyone who remains calm under these circumstances just doesn't understand what is happening."[2] People with anxiety disorders, by contrast, feel severe anxiety, and they feel it much of the time. Aside from OCD, the main categories of anxiety disorders are:

- *Phobias*, which are irrational fears of an object or situation, such as snakes or heights.

- *Panic disorder* (PD), in which feelings of extreme dread strike unexpectedly. The feelings are accompanied by physical sensations, such as a pounding heart, sweating, dizziness, and the feeling of having a heart attack.

- *Post-traumatic stress disorder* (PTSD), which is a reaction to a terrifying event. In PTSD, past trauma breaks into the person's present-day life. This may be in flashbacks or nightmares. The person also exists in a state of hyperalertness and is emotionally numb.

- *Generalized anxiety disorder* (GAD), in which the person worries seriously about many things much of the time.

IS IT FEAR OR ANXIETY?

Fear and anxiety are similar emotions, and the words are sometimes used interchangeably. But fear usually involves an immediate threat. It is a short-term response of the brain and body.[3] For example, our early human ancestors must have felt intense fear when a saber-toothed tiger ran at them. With anxiety, the cause is less immediate and specific. Anxiety builds more slowly and lasts longer.[4] A young woman suddenly promoted to a top position in a big company would probably experience a general uneasiness, or anxiety, about all her new responsibilities.

THE ANXIETY "EDGE"

A certain amount of anxiety can be beneficial. For example, it encourages us to prepare. The athlete anxiously awaiting the biggest competition of his or her life will train hard and be well rested. The shy student anxious about having to give an oral report to the class will rehearse it many times. Anxiety allows us to be alert and focused on what we are doing. It gives us an edge. This is true during both preparation and the actual event.

Anxiety allows us to be alert and focused on what we are doing. It gives us an edge.

Anxiety before performances is exceedingly common. Young music students typically have a bad case of the jitters before recitals. Surprisingly, so do world-famous pianists who trot the globe giving concerts. A certain amount of anxiety helps the performer to be intensely focused and give an exciting performance.

A famous graph from 1908 (see chart on facing page) shows how performance improves with an increase of anxiety. But this occurs only up to a point. Beyond that point, if anxiety continues to increase, performance declines.[5] For the pianist, too much anxiety can result in shaking hands and memory lapses. For the public speaker, too much anxiety can lead to a cracking voice and a lost train of thought. Both may end up focusing on their discomfort instead of what they are trying to communicate.

FIGHT OR FLIGHT

Whenever humans or other higher animals detect danger, their senses send signals to two parts of the brain. One set goes by a roundabout route to the cerebral cortex, the thinking part of the brain. The cerebral cortex is the gray matter in folds on the top of the brain. That part eventually interprets what is

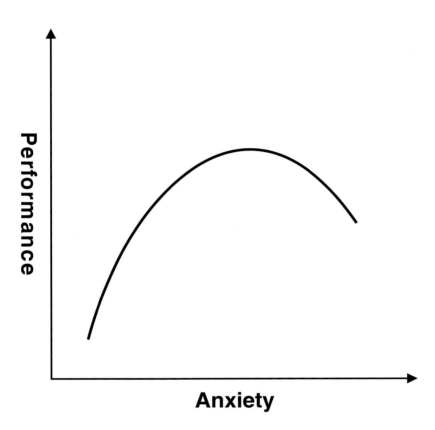

This 1908 chart shows the relationship between anxiety and performance. Anxiety improves performance up to a point. However, after that point, anxiety negatively impacts performance.

happening. It may explain that when you stepped off the curb to cross a one-way street, a bicycle messenger going the wrong way almost flattened you. But before the thinking part of the brain gives meaning to the sights and sounds, the other set of signals has shot directly to the amygdala. The amygdala is an almond-shaped cluster of cells deep in the brain that triggers the fear response. Before you size up the situation consciously, the body reacts in what is called the "fight-or-flight" response. Hormones are released into the body. One of these, adrenaline, pours from the adrenal glands, giving us a jolt of energy. The heart pumps faster, and the lungs work harder. Our perception sharpens. Unnecessary functions like digestion stop, and we are capable of feats of strength unthinkable at other times. All this adds up to our being prepared to either fight or flee. In the above scenario, you leap back up onto the curb before you understand what is happening. After you do understand and calm down, the anxiety response may be turned off.

Many thousands of years ago, the flight-or-fight response helped our ancestors survive predators. In our world today, though, physical dangers are relatively rare. Instead, it is internal, psychological dangers that are widespread. Yet our brains, which are wired to detect danger outside ourselves, remain ready to interpret all danger as physical.[6] We experience fight-or-flight responses to emotional stress. As one psychiatrist expresses it, "We work ourselves up for aggressive physical action when all we do is sit and stew."[7] Bodily reactions to psychological stressors are an important factor in anxiety disorders.

INCREASED VISIBILITY

Since the late 1970s, great strides have been made in understanding anxiety disorders. The major role played by the brain in these disorders becomes ever clearer. This understanding helps those who suffer from an anxiety disorder to not blame themselves. The disorder is not their fault. They are not simply

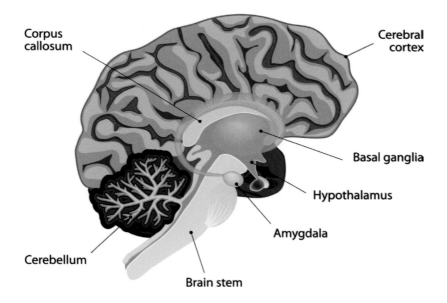

Corpus callosum

Cerebral cortex

Basal ganglia

Hypothalamus

Amygdala

Cerebellum

Brain stem

Humans' fight-or-flight response affects two parts of the brain: the cerebral cortex and the amygdala.

lazy or weak in character. They are not failures in life if they have not been able to overcome their symptoms alone, through sheer strength of will. Yet even today, some people with anxiety disorders feel shame and hide their illness. They may even succeed at concealing it from their closest family members and friends. This only works to their disadvantage. They may end up suffering for many years, or a lifetime, without treatment. In addition, anxiety disorders that have gone many years without treatment are harder to treat.[8]

Many people with anxiety disorders, though, no longer feel a great need to hide their symptoms. Writers admit to all kinds of mental disorders in their memoirs. Celebrities do so in the press. Stories about OCD have made it onto television and into popular magazines. The character Jack Nicholson played in the 1997 hit movie *As Good As It Gets* suffers from OCD.[9] After the terrorist attacks of September 11, 2001, *Time* magazine had a cover story about anxiety disorders.[10] Articles about PTSD, especially as suffered by soldiers who served in the wars in Iraq and Afghanistan, have become more common.

The best news of all is that good treatments for anxiety disorders are finally available. The most effective have been found to be a combination of medications and cognitive-behavioral therapy (CBT). With proper treatment, most patients with anxiety disorders show significant improvement. Many do even better than that.

ANXIETY DISORDERS IN HISTORY

D escriptions of what we today call anxiety disorders appear throughout written history. The first known descriptions were by the Greeks around the fifth century B.C. People who studied science and medicine at that time believed that these disorders were naturalistic, meaning that they could be explained by science. However, in this civilization as well as in the ancient cultures of Egypt and Mesopotamia, people also accepted supernatural explanations for illnesses. For example, people with mental illnesses or disorders were often believed to be possessed by demons or evil spirits or to be under the influence of witchcraft.

The Greek physician Hippocrates (460–377 B.C.) believed that the body contained four humors, or fluids. They were black bile, yellow bile, blood, and phlegm. Each humor was different from the others and was hot or cold and moist or dry. Hippocrates believed that diseases were caused by the body's having too much of one of these humors. For a healthy body, the humors had to be in proper balance. Therefore, disease was "cured" by draining off the humor that was overly abundant.

For example, bloodletting was used to drain off excess blood. What we now call obsessive-compulsive disorder was thought to be a type of depression, which was caused by too much black bile. It was treated with laxatives.[1]

Surprisingly, these beliefs were widespread until about the 1700s. This period included both the Middle Ages (A.D. 500–1500) and the supposedly enlightened Renaissance (A.D. 1300–1600). Yet "witches" were still being burned at the stake during the Renaissance. More accused witches were probably burned in the fifteenth through the seventeenth centuries than during the entire Middle Ages.[2]

In the centuries that followed, great advances were made in the study of the nervous system. Mental problems were now seen as imbalances in the brain and nervous system. No longer were they believed to be caused by imbalances in the body's four humors.[3] Psychotherapy, in which doctor and patient talk to each other, was introduced in the late 1800s.

In the twentieth century, the theories of the Viennese psychiatrist Sigmund Freud (1856–1939) took center stage. Freud believed that mental illness was caused by unresolved conflicts buried deep in the mind, such as the conflict between sexual urges and moral behavior. Many of these conflicts were thought to date back to childhood. Through psychoanalysis, Freud believed these conflicts could be brought into the conscious mind, where they could then be resolved. Psychoanalysis is long-term, intensive therapy—often five sessions a week. In it, the patient's past is examined in great detail.

One path that psychoanalysis uses to access the patient's unconscious mind is free association. The patient says anything that comes to mind. Nothing—no matter how embarrassing— is screened out. Another path to the unconscious is analysis of the patient's dreams.

In the latter third of the twentieth century, psychiatric thought did a turnaround. Mental illnesses came to be seen as

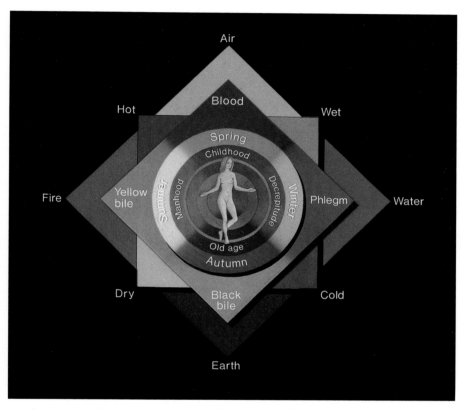

In ancient times physicians believed that illness was a result of an imbalance in the four humors, shown in this chart.

having a stronger basis in biology, as opposed to being based on problems in the patient's upbringing. Psychoanalysis diminished in importance. However, other forms of psychotherapy that grew out of psychoanalysis have continued to be very popular. For most anxiety disorders, cognitive-behavioral therapy (CBT), a type of psychotherapy, and medication are considered the best treatments. Both medication and CBT can make changes in the brain.

OCD THROUGH THE AGES

Throughout the ages, OCD has been observed in religious communities. In more strictly religious centuries, the urge to blaspheme (insult or curse God) was probably the most common type of obsession.[4] An early report is given by Saint John Climacus, who lived from A.D. 570–649: A certain monk was troubled for twenty years by horrible temptations to blaspheme. He rejected these urges with abhorrence and vehemence, arming himself against them by fasts, watchings, and great austerities [acts of self-denial]. Yet, his temptations, far from showing any diminution, daily grew more harassing. At length, being quite at a loss to know what to do, he took counsel of a holy monk.[5]

The holy monk counseled him to try to ignore the temptations. The troubled monk was lucky in his choice of a counselor. Often, the clergy considered people with obsessions to be "witches" or "demons" and ordered that these people be hunted down and tortured or killed.

Later in the Middle Ages, a Christian text gave the following advice: "When you feel that you can in no way put down these thoughts, cower down under them like a poor wretch and a coward overcome in battle, and reckon it to be a waste of time for you to strive any longer against them. Feel as though you are hopelessly defeated."[6]

Sigmund Freud was the father of psychoanalysis. He believed that mental illness is often a result of events in a person's early life.

Oddly, this advice sounds like "flooding," a kind of CBT used today.[7] In flooding, the patient, with the therapist's support, faces the feared thing all at once. Eventually, the anxiety diminishes. Often a patient who has "toughed it out" feels less fear in the future.

> *In flooding, the patient, with the therapist's support, faces the feared thing all at once. Eventually, the anxiety diminishes.*

In the twentieth century, Freudians theorized that OCD was caused by conflicts rooted in the patient's upbringing. One cause was thought to be very strict toilet training.[8] The child might have suffered conflicts over the parents' power and control. Freud thought, however, that psychoanalysis had its limits in explaining OCD. He left the problem to biological research in the future.[9] Today, OCD is understood to be in large part a brain disorder, caused by genetic susceptibility and stress.

HISTORICAL DESCRIPTIONS OF PHOBIAS

The word "phobia" was not used in psychiatry until the mid-1800s. It derives from the Greek *phobos*, meaning terror, fear, or panic. In Greek mythology, Phobos was a god who caused fear and panic among his enemies on the battlefield. Hippocrates was probably one of the first to write a description of phobias. He wrote of one man who feared heights and bridges: "He would not go near a precipice, or over a bridge or beside even the shallowest ditch, and yet he could walk in the ditch itself."[10] Phobias of heights and bridges are still common today.

Through the centuries, phobias have also been described in literature. William Shakespeare (1564–1616) described a cat phobia in *The Merchant of Venice*: "Some, that are mad if they behold a cat."[11] The seventeenth-century English clergyman

An irrational and persistent fear of heights is known as acrophobia.

Robert Burton described the condition we now call agoraphobia, which can involve the fear of leaving home. Burton mentions one man who would "not walk alone from home, for fear he would swoon, or die."[12] Burton also tells of a man with what we now call social phobia: "He dare not come in company, for here he should be misused, disgraced, overshoot himself in gesture or speeches or be sick; he thinks everyman observes him."[13]

For the treatment of phobias, Freud saw that psychoanalysis could not offer a cure: "One can hardly ever master a phobia if one waits till the patient lets the analysis influence him to give it up." Instead, patients make progress only when they can be persuaded to "go about alone and struggle with the anxiety."[14] This sounds like exposure therapy, a type of CBT used today, in which patients face up to the things they fear.

A MODERN NAME FOR "BATTLE STRESS"

War has always left its mark on soldiers. In Homer's *Iliad*, dating from the eighth century B.C., Achilles suffered severe battle stress in the Trojan War.[15] In the United States, researchers began studying battle stress after the Civil War. Since then, it has been called many names, such as shell shock, battle fatigue, combat fatigue, and war neurosis. These conditions were alike in more ways than they were different. In the 1970s, doctors treating Vietnam War veterans began to notice that they had clusters of symptoms in common.One symptom was having the trauma the veterans had suffered break into their present lives in flashbacks and nightmares. Other symptoms were feeling hyperalert to danger and emotionally distant from loved ones. In 1980 post-traumatic stress disorder (PTSD) was first listed in the third edition of the manual used by psychiatrists to diagnose mental disorders, the *DSM-III*. Its full title is the

Many soldiers suffer from post-traumatic stress disorder. Iraq war veteran Zach Choate leads a protest against the redeployment of troops diagnosed with PTSD.

Diagnostic and Statistical Manual of Mental Disorders. Today, a newer edition, the *DSM-V*, is in use.[16]

The symptoms of Vietnam vets have been noted by psychiatrists to be surprisingly like those of a combat veteran in a Shakespeare play.[17, 18] The play is *Henry IV, Part I*; the wife of battle-worn Harry Hotspur is talking. The symptoms of what we now call PTSD are noted on in parentheses:

O, my good lord, why are
you thus alone?   (Withdrawal from loved ones)

For what offense have I this
fortnight been A banish'd
woman from my
Harry's bed?   (Loss of intimacy and pleasure)
. . . .

In thy faint slumbers I by
thee have watch'd,   (Insomnia)

And heard thee murmur
tales of iron wars,   (Nightmares)

Speak terms of manage to
thy bounding steed,   (Reliving combat)

Cry "Courage! to the field!" . . . .
Thy spirit within thee hath
been so at war, And thus hath
so bestirr'd thee in thy sleep,
That beads of sweat have
stood upon thy brow,   (Night sweats)

Like bubbles in a late-
disturbed stream,
And in thy face strange
motions have appear'd,   (Reliving trauma)
. . . .
Some heavy business
hath my lord in hand, And I
must know it, else he loves
me not.[19]   (Withdrawal from loved ones)

Throughout history, soldiers who break down in battle have been unjustly thought of as cowards. Today, though, we understand that biology plays a major role in PTSD, as in other anxiety disorders. Severe trauma causes changes in the brain. The brain is then primed to overreact to future stress. Today, it is believed that any soldier in combat long enough would develop PTSD.[20]

Since the 1980s, PTSD has been studied in a wide variety of traumas. Examples are sexual abuse and natural disasters, such as earthquakes. The terrorist attacks of September 11, 2001, have naturally become a major focus of PTSD research in the past decade.

WHAT IS OCD?

A young psychologist named Dr. S is on his way to take an exam. The streets are not busy, and he is obeying the speed limit. Although everything is going normally, his mind is suddenly swirling with terrible thoughts:

> While in reality no one is on the road, I'm intruded with the heinous thought that I *might* have hit someone. . . a human being! God knows where such a fantasy comes from.

> I think about this for a second and then say to myself, "That's ridiculous. I didn't hit anybody." Nonetheless, a gnawing anxiety is born. An anxiety I will ultimately not be able to put away until an enormous emotional price has been paid.

He tries to reason his way out of these thoughts. He says to himself:

Well, if I hit somebody while driving, I would have *felt* it." This brief trip into reality helps the pain dissipate…but only for a second. Why? Because the gnawing anxiety that I really did commit the illusionary accident is growing larger—so is the pain.

The pain is a terrible guilt that I have committed an unthinkable, negligent act. At one level, I know this is ridiculous, but there's a terrible pain in my stomach telling me something quite different. . . .The attack is now in full control. Reality no longer has any meaning.[1]

He finds himself swept up and carried away by these dark thoughts. He is especially worried about how his parents will react to his being a "criminal." Dr. S. starts to envision his trial and wishes for the jury to be lenient with his punishment.

He finds himself swept up and carried away by these dark thoughts.

The only thing that Dr. S. can think of to rid himself of his tormenting thought is to check to see if he really did hit someone. He drives back five miles to where the "accident" might have occurred. Seeing nothing, he again heads for his exam. But then the thought gnaws at him that maybe he did not go back far enough. He turns the car around and drives back even farther, and then turns again toward school.

Suddenly, though, he thinks that maybe the body was there but he did not see it because his car catapulted it into the bushes. This time, as he checks the bushes, a police officer stops to ask what he is doing. Because he feels that admitting what he was doing would be so "embarrassing," he tells the officer that he is on his way to an exam and had to throw up out of nervousness.

Dr. S. arrives late for the exam and is distracted by thoughts of returning to the "accident scene." He checks several more times on his way home. After he finally climbs into bed, he has to get up once to check the fender for blood and again to check the whole body of the car.[2]

WHAT IS OBSESSIVE-COMPULSIVE DISORDER?

Dr. S. has obsessive-compulsive disorder (OCD). The symptoms of OCD are obsessions and/or compulsions. Most patients have both. According to the *DSM-V*, a diagnosis of OCD should be made only when the symptoms are severe. They must cause marked distress or be time consuming. Or they must interfere seriously with the individual's normal routine, work, or relationships with others.[3] The *DSM-V* dedicates a whole chapter to OCD and related disorders, when in earlier editions these disorders were grouped in the chapter on anxiety disorders. This change allows for more detailed explanation of how OCD diagnoses should be made in children, adolescents, adults, and older adults. The *DSM-V* defines obsessions as intrusive, repetitive, or persistent ideas, thoughts, impulses, urges, or images that cause distress and that cannot be suppressed or ignored.[4]

People with OCD often describe the onset of their obsessions in colorful ways. They say the obsessions "jump" or "pop" into their mind or "come out of nowhere." One young patient observed to his psychiatrist that "an obsession is like Freddie, the character in the *Nightmare on Elm Street* movies. Every time people thought that they were finally rid of Freddie, he came *baaaaack* even stronger."[5]

The compulsions in OCD are acts the person feels driven to do to reduce the anxiety caused by obsessions. They are repetitive behaviors such as hand washing, putting things in order, and checking. They can also be mental acts such as praying, counting, or repeating words silently. These compulsive acts must also take up at least an hour of a person's time per day.[6]

An obsession with contamination might result in a compulsion to clean.

CASUAL TALK VS. CLINICAL TALK

OCD obsessions are different from those you hear about in casual conversation. A teenage girl may be described by her friends as being "obsessed" with a certain boy if she merely has a crush on him. It is the same with compulsions. The hard worker who is said to be "compulsive" is probably just a hard worker. In addition, compulsions that are sometimes enjoyable are not a part of OCD. Take, for example, a casino gambler. He may be unable to tear himself away from the gaming table when the only thing left to bet is his house, yet gambling does provide pleasures. There is the glittering nightlife, the rush of winning, the fantasies of success. By contrast, the compulsions of OCD provide a degree of relief from anxiety but do not bring pleasure.

DIAGNOSES

Although OCD is most often diagnosed in adolescence or early adulthood, it can also begin in childhood.[7] Dr. Judith Rapoport, a pioneer in OCD research, describes a two-year-old boy with a compulsion to walk in circles.[8] Boys have been observed to develop OCD earlier than girls. In childhood, the ratio of boys to girls with OCD is about 3 to 2.[9] Some studies have suggested that some children may outgrow OCD.[10] For most people, though, symptoms wax and wane throughout their lives, getting worse during periods of stress. The nature of the obsessions and compulsions may change also. People with OCD have, on average, four different obsessions and 4.8 compulsions during their lives.[11]

PRIMARY CAUSES OF OCD

The primary causes of OCD are thought to be heredity and life stress. The role that genetics plays in who gets OCD has been suggested by studies of twins. Twin studies are of special importance to researchers. This is because they separate the

THE MOST COMMON OBSESSIONS

Description	Examples
Filth, contamination	Fear of catching a disease by shaking someone's hand or touching a door-knob
Harm to others or self, horrific impulses	Fear of causing harm; urges to hurt one's own child
Counting	Believing that you have to do things a certain number of times or count to a certain number to prevent a "disaster"
Order	Intense distress if objects are not in a certain order by size, color, symmetry, etc.
Blasphemy	Urges to shout curses at God or in church
Hoarding	Fear of throwing out objects; a need to collect objects
Sexual imagery	Recurring, unwanted sexual pictures in your mind

THE MOST COMMON COMPULSIONS

Description	Examples
Washing and cleaning	Washing hands many times a day, sometimes until the skin is raw and bleeding; showering for hours at a time
Checking	Checking many times that the door is really locked, that the stove is off, that you did not hit someone on the highway, etc.
Counting	Having to count to a certain number many times, brush your hair a certain number of times, etc.
Asking for reassurance	Asking constantly for reassurance about certain things
Hoarding	Being unable to throw anything out, such as old, broken things and junk mail; having to pick up every bit of trash from the street
Praying	Uncontrollable urges to repeat prayers many times

effects of genetics and environment on human development. They help to answer questions in the old debate about nurture versus nature. Twins grow up in a shared environment, but they may or may not have identical DNA. Identical, or monozygotic, twins develop from a single embryo and have identical genetic material. Fraternal, or dyzygotic, twins develop from two different embryos. Therefore, they are no more alike than any two siblings.

A 1982 trial studied thirty OCD patients who had twin siblings. Half had identical twin siblings and half had fraternal twin siblings. In the group of OCD patients with identical twin siblings, 87 percent of the other twins were found to also have OCD. In the group of OCD patients with fraternal twin siblings, only 47 percent of the other twins also had OCD.[12] Although this study was small, it provides preliminary evidence that OCD is in part genetic.

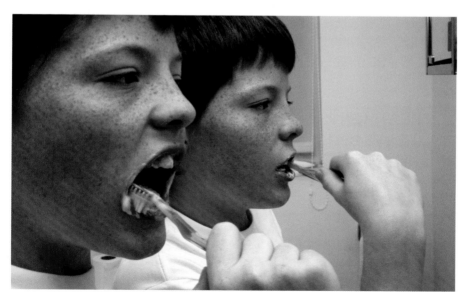

Studies of twins have helped researchers gain a greater understanding of the underlying causes of OCD.

The effect of life stress on the development of OCD has been studied in India by Sumant Khanna and a group of coworkers. The subjects had recently been diagnosed with OCD. The researchers found that in the year before the onset of their illness, the group that developed OCD experienced about twice as many serious stressful events as did a control group.[13] Common stressful events included death and serious illness of family members. Their research suggests that life stress contributes to the development of OCD.

Biological factors are lesser-known causes of OCD. Streptococcal bacterial infections have been found to trigger OCD in children. It is likely, though, that this happens only in children with a genetic predisposition to OCD.[14] Nowadays, university medical centers that treat children with OCD look for antibodies to strep bacteria. If the antibodies are present, the children are treated with antibiotics, and they improve. In addition, brain injuries have been found to lead to OCD. These have included trauma to the head and carbon monoxide poisoning. Brain scans have shown injury to the basal ganglia, a part of the brain that is known to be overactive in people who have OCD.[15]

TREATMENTS FOR OCD

Since the 1970s, great strides have been made in treating OCD. Medications have been developed to restore the brain's normal levels of neurotransmitters. Neurotransmitters are chemicals that carry messages between neurons in the brain. A deficiency of neurotransmitters may cause a serious disorder. The disorder may be in thought, mood, or behavior. Behavior therapy is another treatment for OCD. One type of behavior therapy is called exposure with response prevention. In this commonly used therapy, a patient is exposed to whatever triggers his OCD. For example, someone who is obsessed with cleaning would gradually be exposed to increasing amounts of dirt, while having to wait increasingly longer periods of time before cleaning up. Over time, this kind of behavior therapy can decrease the patient's negative response to his or her trigger.

Dr. Ian Osborn, who specializes in treating OCD, estimates that behavior therapy helps up to 80 percent of those who complete treatment. Medication helps about 50–70 percent of patients.[16] Doing both kinds of treatment together tends to be more effective than doing just one or the other.

WHAT ARE PHOBIAS?

Nineteen-year-old Larry had always been shy. He had also always been a very good student and athlete, so no one understood why he quit college without any warning. After he quit, he moved back in with his parents and never wanted to leave the house. He wouldn't talk to anyone about it. He wouldn't talk about it with his father, who was a doctor, but he did finally agree to see a psychiatrist. Slowly, he grew to trust his doctor and told him what had happened. His apartment at school was next door to four "very flirtatious" female students. "They decided I was 'cute,'" he said, "and they just wouldn't let up on me." Larry would try to avoid them by staying late at the library. His roommate soon found out about the situation and started to pester Larry about it.

> Finally, mainly to get my roommate off my back, I said I'd go to the movies with him and two of the girls. I was a nervous wreck the whole time, and when we got back home to our place, my date just sat down on the couch next to me and kissed me. I was so nervous

already, but I felt my heart race, I started to sweat, and I had to run to the bathroom, where I got sick. All I could think about was that—

At this point in the story, Larry became very upset.

I was just totally humiliated by the idea she must have heard me vomiting. I know she did. . . . That was it. I just couldn't go back. I stayed in the bathroom and I could hear them all talking about how I got sick, that I must be sick. I didn't leave the bathroom until the girls finally went home. I quit school the next day. Now I do not go out at all because I'm afraid there are girls in town who might want to date me. If I see them or they see me, I know I'll get sick again.[1]

Larry's psychiatrist diagnosed him with social phobia.

FEAR OF HUMILIATION

Social phobia is a terror of being humiliated. Basically, it is a fear of making a fool of oneself in front of others. For social phobia to be diagnosed, though, the condition must be severe.

THE MOST COMMON SOCIAL PHOBIAS

Fear of:
- *Public speaking*
- *Performing onstage*
- *Urinating in public restrooms*
- *Eating or drinking in front of others*
- *Writing in front of others*
- *Sexual performance*

The anxiety must interfere seriously with the person's work, social life, or daily routine. Exposure to the feared situations must almost always cause anxiety. When the feared situations cannot be avoided, they are suffered through. Although adults and adolescents with social phobia realize that their fears are excessive, children with social phobia may not.[2] Some people with social phobia fear a particular situation. Fear of public speaking or performing is exceedingly common. Other social phobias are fears of eating, drinking, and writing while others may be watching. Some people cannot use public restrooms. Some fear shaking hands with others, knowing that they will see how their hand shakes.

Social phobia can also be generalized. People may fear humiliation in many kinds of social interactions. In severe cases, people with social phobia suffer symptoms almost any time they are around people. Physical symptoms of social phobia can include a rapidly beating heart, tremors, and sweating. In addition, there might be stomach upset or diarrhea and tensing up of muscles. People with social phobia often feel confused. When many of these symptoms occur together, they may constitute a panic attack. Panic attacks will be described more fully in the next chapter.

> *Physical symptoms of social phobia can include a*
> *rapidly beating heart, tremors, and sweating.*

SURVIVAL VALUE

Social phobia is an extreme form of a very common condition—shyness. Shyness affects from 25 to 40 percent of the population, while social phobia affects only a small fraction of that.[3] As anxiety in general has provided survival value for the human species, so has shyness. Throughout evolution, babies have been protected by their "stranger anxiety." Without the ability to defend themselves, they can scream if a stranger tries

Social phobias usually start in the mid-teens and can become completely debilitating without treatment.

to take them away. Similarly, with adults, wariness around strange tribes, groups, or individuals has proved adaptive. There is always the possibility that strangers might be enemies.

ONSET OF SOCIAL PHOBIA

The onset of social phobia typically begins in the mid-teens. Teens who develop it often were very shy as children. The disorder can also begin in early childhood, though.[4] Social phobia rarely develops after the age of twenty-five.[5] The onset of social phobia may be abrupt, after a humiliating experience, as was the case for Larry. Or it may also be slow, worsening gradually over time. Social phobia may last a lifetime, but it often lessens in adulthood. At times of great stress, symptoms may increase.[6] Even today, many people with social phobia suffer without getting treatment. One study revealed that people with social phobia waited an average of seventeen years before they sought treatment.[7] With increasing awareness about the disorder, however, more people are seeking treatment and doing so early on.

CAUSES AND TREATMENT OF SOCIAL PHOBIA

It seems increasingly likely that a predisposition to social phobia is inherited. Animal studies have identified the site of a gene in mice that affects learned helplessness, a trait that people with social phobia have.[8] A Norwegian study has found that identical twins are more likely than nonidentical twins to both have social phobias.[9] In addition to genetics, life stresses and social modeling are thought to contribute to the development of social phobias. Children of suspicious and distrustful parents, for example, might well model those traits.

The two most effective forms of treatment for social phobia are CBT and medications. In the cognitive part of CBT, the patient learns new ways of thinking about social situations. In the behavior part, the patient may be helped to face the feared

COMMON PHOBIAS

Name	Fear of:
Acrophobia	Heights
Agoraphobia	Open spaces, crowds, leaving home
Arachnophobia	Spiders
Claustrophobia	Closed spaces
Cyberphobia	Computers or things related to computers
Pyrophobia	Fire
Technophobia	Technological devices, such as smartphones
Xenophobia	Strangers or foreigners

UNCOMMON PHOBIAS

Name	Fear of:
Bogeyphobia	Bogeymen, demons, or goblins
Coimetrophobia	Cemeteries, funerals, dead bodies
Lipophobia	Getting fat
Phalacrophobia	Becoming bald
Triskaidekaphobia	The number thirteen
Wiccaphobia	Witches and witchcraft

situations. Interestingly, though, repeated exposure to feared situations has not been found to help performance anxieties. The great Shakespearean actor Sir Laurence Olivier is one of many performers who have suffered severe stage fright all their lives.

> ### *In addition to genetics, life stresses and social modeling are thought to contribute to the development of social phobias.*

Antidepressants, antianxiety medications, and beta-blockers may also be used to treat social phobias. Beta-blockers have been found to lessen performance anxiety. By blocking adrenaline, they lessen symptoms like shaking hands and sweating.[10]

SPECIFIC PHOBIAS

Specific phobias are intense fears of things or situations. These fears interfere seriously with a person's life. For someone with a phobia, the object of fear almost always provokes immediate anxiety. If it cannot be avoided, it is endured with dread.[11] One category of phobias is about animals, such as rats, snakes, and spiders. Another group centers around natural phenomena, such as lightning or tornadoes. Some people fear situations like flying in airplanes or being in an enclosed space. Other have a morbid fear of blood, injuries, choking, or catching an illness.

Many of the objects people with phobias fear threatened our early human ancestors. It is easy to see how fears of fire, snakes, heights, and water protected them from danger. Not as easy to understand is how the fear of open spaces (a type of agoraphobia) helped them survive. But people in open meadows had nowhere to run for cover if there was danger. Most of our phobic fears today are exaggerated forms of fears that helped our species to survive.

Phobias of animals like spiders are relatively common.

COMMON SPECIFIC PHOBIA

Type	Examples
Animal	Snakes, spiders, rats, mice, dogs
Natural environment	Tornadoes, thunderstorms, heights, water
Blood/Injection/Injury	Seeing blood or an injury, getting an injection
Situational	Flying, elevators, bridges, public transportation, driving, enclosed places
Other	Choking, vomiting, getting an illness; children's fear of costumed characters

Some people have a fear of clowns and other people in costumes.

ONSET OF PHOBIAS

When children experience the onset of a specific phobia—for example, of dogs—it often disappears over time.[12] Phobias that begin in adolescence or adulthood are more serious. Only about 20 percent of these fade away on their own.[13]

CAUSES AND TREATMENT FOR SPECIFIC PHOBIAS

Specific phobias are thought to be caused by a mixture of genes and experience. A stressful or scary experience often plays a role in the onset. For example, an abused child who was locked in a closet might develop claustrophobia (fear of enclosed spaces). A person who has almost drowned might develop a phobia about water. Social modeling can play a role as well; children may take on the intense fears their parents have. CBT is the main treatment for phobias. In this method, the patient is gradually exposed to the thing that triggers his or her fear until that fear begins to fade. CBT benefits about three-fourths of the patients who undergo it.[14] Psychiatrists may also prescribe antidepressant or antianxiety medications to further help the patient along in his or her treatment.

PANIC ATTACKS AND PANIC DISORDER

Panic attacks bring on a sense of terror that often is accompanied by physical symptoms. These symptoms include shortness of breath, pounding heart, and dizziness. People often describe their panic attacks as feeling like they are going crazy, like they are having a heart attack, or even like they are dying. Some people's panic attacks seem to come out of nowhere, while some people can sense that they are about to have one. A panic attack usually builds to its full intensity in ten to fifteen minutes and rarely last longer than thirty minutes.

Celia's story of a first panic attack is typical. She was a teenager, working at McDonald's:

> As she was handing a customer a Big Mac, she had the worst experience of her life. The earth seemed to open up beneath her. Her heart began to pound, she felt she was smothering…and she was sure she was going to have a heart attack and die. After about twenty minutes of terror, the panic subsided. Trembling, she got in her car, raced home. . . .

The term "panic" comes from the ancient Greeks. Pan, the god of shepherds and flocks, was depicted as half human and half goat.

Since then, Celia has had about three attacks a month. She does not know when they are coming. . . . She always thinks she is going to die.[1]

PANIC AND THE BODY

The word "panic" derives from the ancient Greek word for Pan, the god of shepherds and flocks. Pan was represented as a being with the legs, ears, and horns of a goat. He was thought to strike fear into people.

Panic is an exaggerated or abnormal form of the body's fight-or-flight response. Excess adrenaline that is released in the body causes physical symptoms. These include racing heart, sweating, and trembling. In turn, the physical symptoms are interpreted as signs of a serious ailment—for instance, a heart attack. When that happens, the person becomes even more anxious. A vicious cycle is set into action.

> *Panic is an exaggerated or abnormal form of the body's fight-or-flight response.*

PANIC DISORDERS

Panic disorder (PD) is a mental disorder in which panic attacks occur. They can either come on unexpectedly or be anticipated by the patient. Those who have the attacks worry about having more attacks. This worry often causes significant changes in their behavior.[2] Panic attacks can occur along with other anxiety disorders. People with OCD, PTSD, a phobia, or agoraphobia, for example, may also have panic attacks. Even if they do, they are said to suffer from OCD, PTSD, a phobia, or agoraphobia, although they may suffer from PD in addition to these disorders. For example, people suffering from both panic attacks and agoraphobia are said to have panic disorder with agoraphobia.

AGORAPHOBIA

Panic disorder and agoraphobia used to be diagnosed together, but they are unlinked in *DSM-V*. Where earlier doctors would diagnose a patient as having panic disorder with agoraphobia, panic disorder without agoraphobia, or agoraphobia without history of panic disorder, they now diagnose each disorder separately.

The name "agoraphobia" derives from the ancient Greeks. It is a combination of *phobos*, meaning "fear," and *agora*, meaning "meeting place." It can mean fear of crowds, such as in malls, supermarkets, or office buildings. It can also mean fear of open spaces or of situations from which escape would be difficult. For some people, agoraphobia means fear of leaving home. However, it is something quite different for others—fear of being home alone.

Consider the story of Al, a supervisor at a plant who loved ball games. He suffered from panic disorder with agoraphobia. After his first panic attack in a restaurant, he said:

> It's not what I did but what I didn't do that became important after a while. Because I stopped going to restaurants, theaters, ballparks—and, hey, I loved football. . . . Anyplace I'd had a panic attack, I wouldn't go there again. My whole life became geared to not doing things.[3]

Some people with very severe agoraphobia do not leave their houses for years. There have been agoraphobics who have stayed in their bedrooms for thirty or forty years. People for whom the disorder is less severe, though, may develop crutches. For example, a woman who is afraid to leave home may be able to if a friend goes with her. A young man who is afraid to go out in the daytime may be able to go out after dark.

Some people who suffer from agoraphobia are often afraid to even leave their homes.

ONSET OF PANIC DISORDERS

Stress seems to have a role in setting off both PD and agoraphobia. The person may have experienced negative life changes, such as the death of a loved one, divorce, or serious illness. Or the person may have suffered serious, ongoing financial problems.

Stress seems to have a role in setting off both PD and agoraphobia.

It is increasingly clear, though, that heredity also plays a role. The researcher M. M. Weissman studied twenty-nine pairs of twins of the same sex in which at least one twin suffered from PD. The twins were a mixture of identical and fraternal. With the identical twins, when one twin had panic disorder, the other twin had it 31 percent of the time. With the fraternal twins, when one twin had panic disorder, none of the others did. Although small, Weissman's study gives preliminary evidence that genetics plays a part in PD.[4] Other studies have shown that blood relatives of people with PD are five to ten times more likely than the general population to have panic attacks.[5] However, these studies, unlike Weissman's, do not separate out the effects of heredity and shared home life.

Biological factors can also play a role in PD. Researchers know this because they have stumbled on substances that can bring on panic attacks. Two of these are caffeine and lactic acid.

Panic disorder usually strikes in young adulthood.[6] Women are twice as likely as men to develop it.[7] Similarly, agoraphobia also affects many more women than men. The reason more women are affected is thought to be related to the traditional role of women. Perhaps because most of their time has been spent in the home, they have been more likely to fear public places.

PANIC ATTACK SYMPTOMS[8]

A panic attack is a period of intense fear in which four or more of the following symptoms develop abruptly:

- *Pounding heart or accelerated heart rate*
- *Sweating*
- *Trembling or shaking*
- *Shortness of breath; sensation of smothering*
- *Feeling of choking*
- *Chest pain or discomfort*
- *Nausea or abdominal discomfort*
- *Feeling dizzy, lightheaded, or faint*
- *Feelings of being unreal or detached from oneself*
- *Fear of losing control or going crazy*
- *Fear of dying*
- *Tingling feeling*
- *Chills or hot flashes*

TREATMENT OF PD

Patients with PD generally respond well to treatment. With professional help, patients make progress within a few weeks of starting treatment. Between 70 to 90 percent of patients eventually find that their symptoms are reduced or can be prevented.[9] The first course of treatment for PD is often antianxiety medication. Antianxiety medication reduces the patient's anxiety about panic attacks. This helps reduce the level of anxiety about panic attacks. CBT is another important part of treatment. CBT teaches the patient how to recognize and cope with panic attacks. If he or she knows the signs of a panic attack, the patient will know he or she is not having a heart attack, for example. Deep breathing and other relaxation exercises help the patient bring the physical symptoms of a panic attack under control once they have started

What Is PTSD?

Although the Vietnam War ended more than forty years ago, Dr. Jonathan Shay still treats Vietnam vets for post-traumatic stress disorder (PTSD) at a Veterans Administration hospital near Boston. Over-alertness is one symptom many of his patients share. Some act as though they are still guarding against the enemy:

> I haven't really slept for twenty years. I lie down, but I don't sleep. I'm always watching the door, the window, then back to the door. I get up at least five times to walk my perimeter, sometimes it's ten or fifteen times. There's always something within reach, maybe a baseball bat or a knife, at every door. I used to sleep with a gun under my pillow, another under my mattress. . . .You made me get rid of them when I came into the program here. . . .

> Sometimes I think about them—I want to have a gun in my hands so bad at night it makes my arms ache. So it's like that until the sun begins to come up, then I can sleep for an hour or two.[1]

Numbness is another symptom Dr. Shay's patients also describe. They say that they feel distant, even from their family and friends:

> At Christmastime, I try to make it perfect for the kids with a big, fresh tree trimmed just right and lots of presents, but it's like I'm watching them through a dirty window. I'm not really there and they're not really there. . . . Maybe none of us is real. It's like I'm wrapped up in some kind of transparent cocoon and everything gets kind of muffled . . . . [2]

Another symptom is having the long-gone war break into their daily lives. This can happen in flashbacks, which are very vivid memories. It can also happen in horrible nightmares. One of Dr. Shay's patients, whom he calls "C.," has hallucinations.

The trauma endured by troops in the recent war in Iraq has also led to many cases of PTSD in returning soldiers.

Hallucinations are sights or sounds that the person believes to be real, but that are not. C. sometimes hallucinates about a soldier he killed. On the day it happened, C. was with a newly arrived soldier who "didn't know anything." They were unloading their helicopter at one of their stops. Suddenly, a North Vietnamese soldier jumped out of the bushes. With his AK-47, he cut off the new soldier's head. C. responded by emptying the clip of his M-16 into the enemy soldier. Then, in an act of war rage, he tore off the enemy soldier's head.

In the decades since the war, C. has celebrated few Thanksgiving or Christmas dinners alone with his family. An uninvited guest usually appears—that dead Vietnamese soldier or his head. In the presence of the hallucinated soldier, C. has also attempted suicide several times.[3]

WHAT IS POST-TRAUMATIC STRESS DISORDER?

People who suffer from PTSD have been exposed to a terrifying event. They felt intense fear, horror, or helplessness. Afterward, they experience the three types of symptoms described above:

1. They are hyperalert. They may describe this as feeling jumpy or on guard against another terrifying event.
2. They feel a deadening of normal human emotions. They may have trouble loving, or accepting love from, others.
3. They can't help reliving the past trauma. They will likely have flashbacks and nightmares. They might also experience hallucinations.

When these symptoms seriously interfere with a person's life, a stress disorder is diagnosed. If the symptoms disappear in less than a month, the condition is called acute stress disorder (ASD).[4] If the symptoms last for more than one month, PTSD is diagnosed.[5] Symptoms of PTSD usually begin to appear within three months of the trauma. Occasionally, they develop years later.

ONSET OF PTSD

Degree of exposure to a traumatic event is one risk factor for PTSD. The severity of the trauma is another. The fact that a trauma is caused by human beings—instead of being a natural occurrence, like a tidal wave—is still another. After the terrorist attacks of September 11, 2001, when commercial airplanes were flown into the World Trade Center and the Pentagon, the group of people most at risk for developing PTSD were those most directly involved. These included the rescue workers and people who ran for their lives from the burning buildings and falling debris. Hundreds of neighborhood children also witnessed people leaping to their deaths from the upper stories of the trade center. Thousands more people also lost loved ones or witnessed the horror firsthand.

It is likely that the great majority of people directly involved never developed full-blown PTSD. From past studies, researchers predict that about 75 percent of people exposed to a trauma

Some of those who survived the 9/11 attacks experienced symptoms of PTSD in the months and years afterward.

never develop PTSD. However, a small number who merely watched the horror on television probably will. This can be explained in part, at least, by another risk factor: having suffered extreme stress before. Combat veterans from Vietnam who had previously endured severe stress—such as childhood sexual abuse—were more likely to suffer from PTSD than those who had not.

Developing PTSD may be due in part to a breakdown in the system the body uses to deal with stress. This system is extremely complicated; we are only beginning to understand pieces of it. As explained in chapter one, the amygdala coordinates the body's fear response. Researchers theorize that fear responses are etched onto the amygdala. These etched memories may cause people to overreact in the future to situations that are not that frightening. In people with PTSD, even a slight reminder of the original trauma may cause a fear response.[6]

Researchers theorize that fear responses are etched onto the amygdala. These etched memories may cause people to overreact in the future to situations that are not that frightening.

There may also be a breakdown in the production of hormones. When a threat is perceived, the organism prepares to fight or flee. Stress hormones, such as adrenaline, surge through the body. Cortisol, another hormone, works to shut down unnecessary activities like digestion. But cortisol has an additional job. It shuts down the production of stress hormones after they are no longer needed.

Dr. Rachel Yehuda, a specialist in post-traumatic stress, theorizes that in PTSD, production of cortisol shuts down too early.[7] Therefore, there may not be enough cortisol in the system to shut down the production of other stress hormones. They may continue to pour into the body long after they are

First responders to a traumatic event, like the ones shown here after the shooting at Sandy Hook Elementary School, are at elevated risk for developing PTSD.

needed. Research suggests that this is the case. People who did eventually develop PTSD have been tested as having lower levels of cortisol after a trauma than those who did not.[8]

DIFFERENT KINDS OF TRAUMAS

People can develop PTSD if they have been exposed to a trauma that is not war- or terrorism-related. Other kinds of human-made violence can lead to PTSD, such as torture, abuse, sexual abuse, rape, and witnessing a school shooting. Accidents such as plane crashes can also lead to PTSD. Natural disasters such as earthquakes, volcanoes, and floods also commonly lead to PTSD. PTSD affects both survivors and rescue workers. Although we tend to think of the tragedies seen in the news as causing PTSD, personal traumas like car accidents can also cause the disorder.

TREATING PTSD

Medication and CBT are the most important treatments for PTSD. Medication is used to help calm the patient. CBT is used to gradually desensitize the patient to their memories, which lessens their power over the patient. Therapy also helps the patient live with his or her memories in new, less negative, ways.

GENERALIZED ANXIETY DISORDER

T here are other types of anxiety disorders, such as generalized anxiety disorder (GAD), anxiety disorder due to a general medical condition, and substance-induced anxiety disorder. GAD is the best known of the other anxiety disorders. While everyone feels anxious from time to time, a person with GAD feels anxious a lot of the time and about many things.[1] A person with GAD can be thought of as a "worrier who torments himself by incessantly searching for what can go wrong in life."[2]

GAD DIAGNOSIS

According to the *DSM-V*, GAD is marked by excessive anxiety. The worry is over a number of things and is hard to control. It significantly affects a person's life. For a diagnosis of GAD to be made, some of the following symptoms must also be present:

- Feeling keyed up or restless
- Being easily tired
- Having trouble concentrating
- Feeling irritable

- Having tense muscles
- Having trouble sleeping[3]

Some common worries of a person with GAD include health, family members, money matters, and work.

When GAD begins in childhood, children often worry about their performance at school and in sports. But they may worry about many other things as well, such as earthquakes or other natural disasters. They tend to need constant reassurance about their anxieties.[4] In adolescence, the focus shifts somewhat to being accepted by one's peers.

E. B. White, the author of *Stuart Little* and *Charlotte's Web*, used to say that he had been "born scared":

> The normal fears and worries of every child were in me developed to a high degree; every day was an awesome prospect. I was uneasy about practically everything: the uncertainty of the future, the dark of the attic, the . . . discipline of school, the transitoriness of life, the mystery of the church and of God, the frailty of the body, the sadness of afternoon...the distant challenge of love and marriage, the far-off problem of a livelihood. I brooded about them all, lived with them day by day.[5]

White said that writing helped to lessen his anxieties. That is why he started writing at a young age.

CAUSES, ONSET, AND TREATMENT

Some research suggests that GAD runs in families.[6] The reason for this is probably not only genetics, but also the environment. Young members of a family learn anxious behavior from their elders. GAD usually begins to affect people in childhood or adolescence. But it can also begin in adulthood.[7] It is an ongoing condition that tends to worsen at times of stress. The main treatments for GAD are medications and cognitive therapy.

E. B. White said writing was his way of coping with his many worries and anxieties.

Antianxiety medication is sometimes used in the beginning of treatment. Antidepressants can be used without the risk of dependency. With cognitive therapy, the patient can learn to substitute positive thoughts for negative ones. Deep breathing and relaxation exercises are also very helpful, as is a regular program of exercise.

ANXIETY CAUSED BY MEDICAL CONDITIONS

Another type of anxiety disorder is the result of a medical problem. It is easy to understand how sick people may become anxious about their health. Yet that is not the situation here. An anxiety disorder due to a general medical condition is a physiological result of a medical problem. For example, the anxiety disorder can be caused by an overactive thyroid gland. That is what happened to Millicent.

An anxiety disorder due to a general medical condition is a physiological result of a medical problem.

The first time Millicent felt strange sensations was at work at the video store. Her heart began to pound, she became short of breath, and she started to sweat heavily. She felt closed in and longed to run outside. But because she was alone in the store, she had to stay. Although she was only twenty-four, she thought that she might be dying.

Over the next few weeks, she noticed other symptoms. She was hungry all the time yet lost ten pounds. She would fall asleep watching TV—something that never used to happen.

She went to a doctor, who noticed other symptoms: Her eyes bulged and she squirmed in her chair. The doctor diagnosed an overactive thyroid gland. The thyroid gland, at the base of the neck, releases hormones that affect metabolism. With treatment, Millicent's overactive thyroid was controlled within two months. Her anxiety disappeared completely.[8] This type of anxiety disorder is cured when the underlying medical condition is successfully treated.

ANXIETY CAUSED BY SUBSTANCES

Substance-induced anxiety disorder results from exposure to certain substances. Common examples are alcohol, marijuana, and amphetamines. But they can also be toxins people are accidentally exposed to. Oddly, the disorder can be caused in two ways that seem to be opposites. One way is by intoxication with a substance. The other is by withdrawal from it. The disorder is diagnosed only when the anxiety is worse than would be expected in states of intoxication or withdrawal.

Substance-induced anxiety disorder can stem from overindulging in substances like alcohol.

Bonita's substance-induced anxiety disorder was caused by intoxication. She had only recently arrived on campus for her first year of college. She had been raised as a strict Catholic. Before moving away from home, the only alcohol she had tasted was at Communion. Now she found herself in rush week for sororities.

At a party for new pledges, she drank beer and then smoked marijuana. Suddenly, her head began to feel tight and her lungs hurt. She became convinced that she was going to die. She tried to run away, but her legs were rubbery and would not carry her. She felt panicky, certain that she was dying or going mad. Finally, she was taken to the hospital by her friends. As soon as the alcohol and marijuana were out of Bonita's system, she was fine.[9]

SUBSTANCES THAT CAN CAUSE SUBSTANCE-INDUCED ANXIETY DISORDER

Type	Example
Alcohol	Vodka, rum, beer, wine
Amphetamines	Ritalin, methamphetamine
Caffeine	Coffee, tea
Hallucinogens	LSD
Inhalants	Paint thinner, liquid eraser, glue
Toxins	Some cleaning agents, paint removers
Marijuana	

A WARNING ABOUT SELF-DIAGNOSIS

Diagnosing anything, including anxiety disorders, is a task that should be left to qualified professionals. They have been trained to tell the difference between anxiety disorders and other illnesses. They can pinpoint the clusters of symptoms that define each anxiety disorder, and they can also judge their severity. Medical students are known for convincing themselves that they have the diseases they are studying. The same thing often happens when people who aren't medical professionals read about diseases and disorders. This can be especially true when reading about GAD. That's because everyone feels anxious sometimes, even though they most likely do not have an anxiety disorder. Diagnosing is too tricky to perform on oneself and should be done only by a person who is qualified to treat mental disorders.

TREATING ANXIETY

The two main treatments for anxiety disorders are medication and cognitive-behavioral therapy (CBT). A combination of these two treatments is what tends to work best for most patients. First the doctor may prescribe medication such as an antidepressant or an antianxiety drug. The medication will help put the patient in a better frame of mind to do the work of the next step, CBT. CBT is used to change the patient's negative behaviors or patterns of thought and to help him or her cope with anxiety.

In some cases, psychotherapies other than CBT might be helpful to a patient. Some of these include family therapy, group therapy, and traditional talk therapies.

MEDICATIONS FOR ANXIETY

Antidepressants

Antidepressants work to restore the natural levels of chemicals in the brain. These chemicals, called neurotransmitters, carry signals from one neuron, or nerve cell, to another. They transmit the messages across the spaces between neurons called

Taking an antidepressant may help a person suffering from anxiety by improving her mindset before starting therapy.

synapses. Because it often takes a few weeks to feel better after beginning antidepressant medication, it is likely that it takes time for the brain to respond to the increased levels of neurotransmitters.[1]

Four classes of antidepressants are available today.[2] Each affects different neurotransmitters in different ways. The SSRIs (selective serotonin reuptake inhibitors) bring about higher levels of the neurotransmitter serotonin. A deficiency of neurotransmitters such as serotonin is thought to contribute to anxiety disorders. The SSRIs have relatively few side effects. They can cause sleeplessness, jitteriness, and nausea, but these often go away in a few weeks. Prozac and Zoloft are two very popular SSRIs.

The TCAs (tricyclic antidepressants) affect two neurotransmitters: serotonin and dopamine. The TCAs can have unpleasant side effects, such as weight gain and constipation, which may not go away. The MAOIs (monoamine oxidase inhibitors) inhibit the breakdown of three types of neurotransmitters. By doing so, they ensure higher levels of these chemicals in the brain. People on MAOIs cannot eat certain types of food that interact with the medication. The fourth category of antidepressants is the atypical, a group of miscellaneous antidepressants. Each works in a unique way, on multiple transmitters.

ANTIDEPRESSANTS USED FOR ANXIETY DISORDERS

Type	Trade Name	Generic Name
SSRIs	Prozac	fluoxetine
	Zoloft	sertraline
	Paxil	paroxetine
	Luvox	fluvoxamine
	Celexa	citalopram
TCAs	Anafranil	clomipramine
	Tofranil	imipramine
MAOIs	Nardil	phenelzine
Atypical	Effexor	venlafaxine

Antianxiety Medication

Antianxiety medications work on the central nervous system. They make the patient feel relaxed and peaceful. They are sometimes used along with exposure therapy, as patients learn to face their fears. Because the group called benzodiazepines can be addictive, they are prescribed with caution. It is unlikely that doctors would give them to patients who might abuse alcohol or drugs. Buspirone, another kind of antianxiety agent, is not addictive. It can be taken for several months at a time.

GETTING A PRESCRIPTION

Only medical doctors can prescribe medication. Psychiatrists are medical doctors who specialize in treating mental disorders. Although psychologists and social workers are not able to

A prescription for antidepressants or antianxiety medication must be obtained from a medical doctor like a licensed psychiatrist.

ANTIANXIETY MEDICATIONS

Type	Trade Name	Generic Name
Benzodiazepines	Xanax	alprazolam
	Ativan	lorazepam
	Klonopin	clonazepam
	Valium	diazepam
Other	BuSpar	buspirone

prescribe medicine, they may work closely with a psychiatrist, who can. Doctor and patient may have to experiment with a number of different medications. Each person reacts uniquely to medications. Through trial and error—and patience—medications can usually be found that are effective, with few side effects.

CBT WITH OBSESSIVE-COMPULSIVE DISORDER

In the cognitive part of CBT, patients learn to think in new ways. The therapist helps the patient interrupt, and then change, negative thought patterns. Dr. Tamar Chansky, who treats children with OCD, recommends naming the OCD. She tells young patients to imagine the OCD as being outside themselves. Think of it as a bully and boss it back! This approach assures children that the OCD is not their fault.[3] Instead, it is a kind of misfiring in the brain, a mechanical glitch.[4] The messages OCD sends are like junk mail from the brain.[5] Dr. Ian Osborn has similar advice. He suggests waving off an obsession like an "obscenity shouted by a harmless drunk."[6] The behavior part of CBT is based on a simple reaction of all animals. It is called habituation. If you touch a snail's head once, it will pull back into its shell. However, if you touch it again and again, it will gradually get used to the unpleasant stimulus. Eventually, it will not withdraw its head anymore.[7]

The therapist helps the patient interrupt, and then change, negative thought patterns.

Behavior therapy typically involves homework. Dr. Osborn has his OCD patients begin by keeping a diary for a few days. In it they identify their obsessions and compulsions. The diary is in the form of a chart, with data entered into columns. Patients enter the time of day each obsession occurred and what they were doing at the time. Then they enter the compulsions performed to lessen the anxiety. Next, they rate the severity of the obsessions and compulsions. Finally, they note how long they lasted.[8]

After this diary has been completed, doctor and patient rank the obsessions. Which caused the most anxiety? Which the least? Only now is it time for the patient to begin the exposure part of the therapy. Patients with a terror of contamination, the most common kind of OCD, will touch something they consider slightly dirty. They will not be allowed to wash for a short time. As the therapy progresses, the dirt will get dirtier and the time before washing will grow longer. This is called exposure with response prevention. Dr. Osborn has found that for a compulsive hand washer, twenty or thirty hours of behavior therapy is usually enough.[9] The patient will not be cured of OCD but will have the symptoms well under control.

CBT WITH SOCIAL PHOBIA

Patients with social phobia usually benefit by learning to recognize their unrealistic, negative patterns of thought. Dr. John Marshall, who heads the Anxiety Disorders Clinic at the

Keeping a journal will help both therapist and patient learn more about what triggers anxiety.

University of Wisconsin, helps patients identify instances of bad logic. His categories of bad logic, followed by examples, are listed below.[10]

- Mind reading: "I know everyone in that group thinks I'm a jerk."

- Fortune telling: "Before I finish playing my recital piece, everyone will walk out."

- Predicting catastrophe: "I know I'll mess up on the test, and then I'll flunk out."

- All-or-nothing thinking: "They'll either love me or hate my guts."

- Selective remembering: Remembering embarrassing moments and forgetting those when you were a social success.

Dr. Marshall also assigns homework. A graduate student patient had an intense fear of walking into a class where other students were already seated. He imagined that they all watched him enter, thinking terrible things about him. Dr. Marshall had him observe the other students each time he entered. How many were actually interested in his entrance? What did their expressions convey? How did they respond to other students who entered the room? The patient learned that in reality the other students showed little interest when anyone entered. His anxiety had been based on faulty thinking.[11] When he fully understood this, his anxiety diminished.

CBT WITH PANIC ATTACKS AND PHOBIAS

Patients having panic attacks often think they are dying or going crazy. In the cognitive part of CBT, patients learn that these thoughts are self-defeating. They only make the attack worse. In the behavioral part of CBT, patients may be gradually desensitized to the symptoms they associate with panic. Dr. Edward Hallowell has a patient practice running up and down

Talking to a therapist can help a patient look at his or her anxieties in a new way and begin to overcome them.

a flight of stairs enough times to get out of breath. The object is to learn that this symptom, being out of breath, does not necessarily mean a panic attack is coming.The patient will also learn to replace unrealistic thoughts—"This is the beginning of an attack. . . I am going to die"—with realistic ones. In addition, the patient will learn to control the physical symptom with relaxation techniques (discussed below). After the patient has learned to handle one physical symptom of panic, another, such as dizziness, is added. Now the patient runs up the flights of stairs and then twirls around until he or she is dizzy. When the patient has learned to control two symptoms through relaxation, a third is added.[12]

Another type of exposure therapy is called flooding. The patient is immersed all at once in the feared thing. With panic attacks, an attack might be purposely brought on in therapy. With the therapist's help, the patient learns to ride it out. Because the body runs out of stress hormones, it can sustain red alert for only so long. Panic attacks usually peak within minutes. After that, the symptoms subside.

Desensitization and flooding are also used to treat phobias. A man with a terror of heights may begin by climbing one floor higher every week. Or he may attempt to confront his fear all at once and take the elevator all the way to the top.[13]

Exposure therapy may also be done purely in the imagination. The patient may imagine, in great detail, climbing one floor higher every day. Computer programs that simulate real-life situations may be used as aids. Exposure in the imagination and virtual reality exposure have a couple of advantages. One is that they can help people who are too afraid to brave their fears in real-life situations. The other is that the confidentiality of patients can be protected. Instead of a therapist accompanying a patient in feared situations—such as riding to the top of a building—the exposure can occur in the therapy office or at the patient's home. Virtual reality exposure has been found to be effective with specific phobias and agoraphobia.[14]

Cognitive behavior therapy can be effective in treating patients with PTSD by helping them to gradually recover memories of the traumatic event, eventually reducing the power of the event.

CBT WITH POST-TRAUMATIC STRESS DISORDER

With post-traumatic stress, CBT is used to expose the patient, gradually, to painful memories. The patient begins telling bits of the story. In time, more and more memories are recovered. By the end of therapy, the patient may have told the whole story many times over. During this time, the therapist helps the patient think about the experiences in less self-defeating ways. For example, patients may be burdened with much more guilt than is appropriate.Virtual reality exposure is also being used with Vietnam vets.[15] Here is how it might work: The veteran flies in a virtual helicopter over Vietnam. The terrains include rice paddies, rivers, jungles, and clearings. As the vet hears the hammer of gunfire and feels the helicopter vibrating, the therapist draws out memories. Patient and therapist work together to recall the traumatic memories. Perhaps the veteran will learn to reframe the experiences, or think of the memories in new, more positive ways. When the traumatic memories are faced head-on, they will lose their power. They will not try to sneak into everyday living, dreams, or nightmares.

RELAXATION TECHNIQUES

It has wisely been said that "an anxious mind cannot exist in a relaxed body."[16] If the body is relaxed, a decrease in anxiety will naturally follow. Two relaxation techniques will be described here. A regular program of exercise is also extremely helpful.

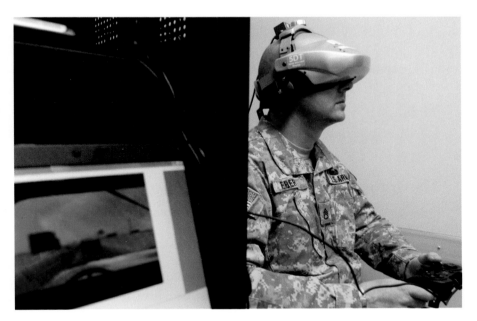

A US soldier wears a virtual-reality headset and holds a video-game-type controller that will be used to treat veterans by simulating the war experience.

Breathing

People who are tense or anxious tend to take quick shallow breaths. Their breathing occurs high up in their chest. This type of breathing can cause bodily changes that then cause more symptoms of anxiety. One such change is constriction of the blood vessels in the brain. This brings on dizziness and feelings of unreality.[17] Deep breathing is associated with relaxation. With practice, the technique will become automatic. Here is one way to do it:

- Lie on your back, with your arms a little away from your body.

- Inhale slowly and deeply through your nose. Let the air all the way down to fill your lower abdomen—feel your stomach rise—and then the bottom of your lungs.

- After you have taken a deep breath, pause for a moment. Then exhale slowly through your nose or mouth. As you exhale, allow your whole body to let go.

These exercises can be done in sets, once or twice a day. Abdominal breathing reduces anxiety and can even reduce symptoms leading to a panic attack.

Muscle Relaxation

Another method of relaxation focuses on muscles from one end of the body to the other. It can be done on your back, along with deep abdominal breathing. Or it can be done in a sitting position. After inhaling, imagine all the tension being released from a group of muscles. You might start with the toes, arches, and heels. You continue like this all the way to the eye muscles, forehead, and scalp.[18] Another method has you clench each group of muscles as hard as you can on the inhale and then release on the exhale.

OTHER THERAPIES

There are other therapies that are helpful at treating anxiety disorders. Family therapy uses the whole family to treat the person with an anxiety disorder. The idea behind this is that a person's anxiety disorder affects his or her whole family and

There are many nontraditional therapies available to people with anxiety disorders. Some veterans suffering from PTSD say that equine therapy, or working with horses, calms their anxieties.

that the family environment can help (or hurt) the patient. Family members learn about the disorder and how to relate positively to the one who is ill. Siblings will often work through feelings of resentment—that is because the sibling who is suffering from the disorder is probably getting most of the parents' attention. Group therapy puts together people with the same disorder. The thinking behind this therapy is that patients can learn from others with similar problems and provide support to one another. These patients also often bond with one another, which is very important for people with PTSD.

In talk therapy, the patient and the doctor have open-ended talks with the goal of having insights to the patient's problems. There are several other types of therapy that are less commonly used, and new therapies are constantly being developed.

ANXIETY, SOCIETY, AND RESEARCH

Anxiety disorders are the most commonly diagnosed mental disorder in the United States. About forty million Americans age eighteen and older are affected by these disorders in a given year.[1] This is about 18 percent of the population.

ANXIETY AND OTHER CONDITIONS

Many people who are diagnosed with an anxiety disorder are also diagnosed with another mental disorder. Having two separately diagnosed mental disorders is called having co-occurring conditions. There are several illnesses that are likely to co-occur with anxiety disorder. Substance abuse is a common co-occurring condition: People with severe anxiety may try to self-medicate with alcohol or drugs. Often, they end up abusing these substances.

Having two separately diagnosed mental disorders is called having co-occurring conditions.

Another co-occurring condition is depression. A woman afraid to leave her house might understandably sink into depression. Without the stimulation of a social life, a job, or being out and about, her world may seem hostile and gray. Similarly, a man tormented with obsessions may despair of ever having the carefree days that his friends seem to be having. Other co-occurring conditions are other anxiety disorders. Certain physical ailments may accompany an anxiety disorder as well. A common co-occurring physical condition is irritable bowel syndrome.

AMERICANS WITH ANXIETY DISORDERS [2]

Type	Percentage of Population with Disorder
OCD	1 percent
Any Phobia	8.7 percent
Social Anxiety	6.8 percent
PD	2.7 percent
PTSD	3.5 percent
GAD	3.1 percent
Any Anxiety Disorder	18 percent

AGE OF ONSET OF ANXIETY DISORDERS [3]

Type	When It Typically Begins
OCD	Adolescence or early childhood
Social Phobia	Childhood or early adolescence; rarely develops after age twenty-five
PD	Young adulthood
PTSD	Any age, including childhood; symptoms usually begin within three months of traumatic event but can begin years later
GAD	Childhood or adolescence, but can begin in adulthood

THE COST OF ANXIETY

Anxiety disorders cost $42.3 billion annually in the United States.[4] This equals about one-third of the nation's $148 billion mental health bill. The costs are to individuals and to society as a whole. Wages are lost when those with anxiety disorders miss work. At work, their productivity decreases. They have to make frequent use of health care services—for both psychiatric and medical treatments. In addition to economic costs, those with anxiety disorders obviously experience a diminished quality of life.

ANXIETY AND CULTURAL DIFFERENCES

It is likely that anxiety disorders are present in all cultures. They are found in developing countries as well as industrialized ones. However, there are definite differences across cultures. For example, people in more relaxed societies—such as Mediterranean cultures—have fewer anxiety disorders than those in less relaxed ones. What constitutes an anxiety disorder also varies across cultures. In some societies, an absolute terror of spirits, magic, and the ghosts of one's ancestors is part of the culture.[5] Scientists would be mistaken to think that a person exhibiting it had a phobia or panic disorder. As another example, in Japan people with social phobia often have an excessive fear of giving offense to others. In our culture, social phobia typically involves an excessive fear of being embarrassed ourselves, rather than offending others.[6]

Anxiety disorders are more common in some parts of the world than others. Some cultures, such as that found in Greece, tend to be more relaxed than others.

RESEARCH ON ANXIETY DISORDERS

Much research is currently focused on anxiety disorders. Brain imaging studies and genetic studies are two major areas of focus.

Brain Imaging

Modern brain-imaging tools allow researchers to see moving pictures of the brain. They can watch the amygdala, the cortex, and other parts of the brain at work. They can watch as their subjects perform particular tasks—for example, a thinking task or responding emotionally to a photograph. The brain scans of those with and without a particular anxiety disorder can then be compared. The researchers can investigate the precise neural circuits involved in different anxiety disorders.

> *Specific anxiety disorders may be associated with different parts of the amygdala. Different parts of the brain may also be associated with specific anxiety disorders.*

Recent studies have focused on pinpointing the specific areas of the brain involved in fear and anxiety. As noted above, the amygdala has been found to coordinate the body's fear response. Specific anxiety disorders may be associated with different parts of the amygdala. Different parts of the brain may also be associated with specific anxiety disorders. Recent studies have found, for example, that the hippocampus, a part of the brain involved in emotion, tends to be smaller in people who suffer from PTSD. Research is under way at the National Institute of Mental Health (NIMH) to sort out this information. Is the small size the result of extreme stress reactions? Or are people with a smaller hippocampus more likely to get PTSD?[7] Imaging studies have also found that people with OCD have less white matter and more gray matter (brain cells) than those without OCD.[8] This makes sense, as people with OCD seem to think too much.

Genetic Mapping
One type of genetic research is genetic mapping. Researchers are trying to locate genes that influence the organism in certain ways. As researchers have located genes that predispose people to physical diseases—such as breast cancer—they are finding genes that predispose people to mental disorders. A gene that has been found to influence fearfulness in mice is thought to play a role in agoraphobia and social phobia.[9] Another type of genetic study is twin research, of the type discussed in the chapters on OCD and PD. Twin studies have suggested that OCD, PD, and also social phobia are in part genetic.[10]

ANXIETY DISORDERS IN MEN AND WOMEN [11]

Type	Gender
OCD	Equally common in males and females
Social Anxiety	Equally common in males and females
PD	Twice as common in females
Specific Phobia	Twice as common in females
GAD	Twice as common in females

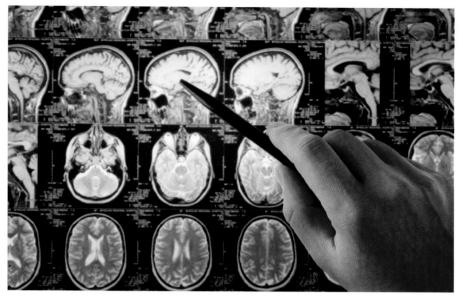

Scientists are now able to study the different areas of the brain to see how they differ in people with anxiety disorders.

LOOKING TO THE FUTURE

Another kind of research is studies that compare treatments. For example, a study might compare how medication and CBT stand up as treatments for anxiety disorders. Does one have better results in the long term? Doing this kind of research helps better treatments and combinations of treatments to be developed. It is also hoped that research studies will enable doctors to predict who might develop anxiety disorders and when. Someday, we might even be able to prevent them.

TOP 10 QUESTIONS AND ANSWERS

Does having an anxiety disorder mean that I am weak?

New understanding of the role that biology plays in anxiety disorders should reassure patients that they are not weak. It is also important to know that without proper treatment, it is almost impossible to "snap out of it" or "get a grip" on their symptoms.

If I have social phobia and am too terrified to talk to boys or girls or go to parties, does this mean that I'll never get married?

People with social phobia do get married, although they tend to do so later in life than others. However, they also tend to have very strong marriages.

Are antidepressants addictive?

No. However, your body does get used to a certain level of the medication. To stop taking a medication, it is usually best to follow doctors' orders for cutting down gradually. Stopping abruptly does not cause a craving, but it could cause depression, agitated sleeping, or other problems.

How long will I have to take antidepressants?

It varies from person to person. It may be for a relatively short time, or it may be for a long time. Many people who take antidepressants are comfortable with the idea that they may take them for the rest of their lives.

What should I do if the medication I am taking for my anxiety causes side effects?

Any medication can cause side effects, including those that are prescribed for anxiety. If you experience side effects, call your doctor right away. Do not stop taking the medication unless the doctor instructs you to do so because stopping some medications abruptly can be harmful.

Don't you have to understand why you do something before you can change it?

Understanding is helpful, but in treating symptoms of anxiety disorders, it is not enough. Changes in the brain are necessary—and those are brought about by medication and CBT.

What are some lifestyle changes I can make to help lessen my anxiety symptoms?

While lifestyle changes alone cannot treat anxiety, together with therapy and/or medication, they can lessen your symptoms. These changes include cutting down on caffeine, eating a healthy diet, getting regular exercise, and trying relaxation techniques, meditation, or yoga.

Do children and teens have different symptoms of PTSD than adults?

Children with PTSD often show symptoms not seen in adults, such as bed-wetting, being unable to talk, or acting out the traumatic event during play. Teens show PTSD symptoms much the same way as do adults.

Should people with PTSD be encouraged to talk about their trauma?

It is important to let a person with PTSD move at his or her own pace and not be pushed to talk about the trauma unless he or she wishes to do so.

What's the difference between being a "neat freak" and having OCD?

First, a person with OCD may have obsessions other than with cleanliness and compulsions other than cleaning. The other important distinction is that someone who has a "neat freak" personality is more comfortable when things are neat, rather than feeling a disruptive level of anxiety about cleaning and cleanliness.

Timeline of Stress and Anxiety

c. 900 BC   Homer's Illiad provides one of literature's earlest d scriptions of PTSD.

c. 400 BC   Ancient Greeks theorize that all disease is caused by the body's humors, a naturalistic explanation.

c. 400 BC   Hippocrates describes phobias and obsessive-compulsive disorder.

c. AD 600   Saint John Climacus documents an early description of OCD.

Middle Ages and

Renaissance The humoral theory of disease is still widespread, as well as supernatural theories that disease is caused by possession by demons or evil spirits.

c. 1700   Mental illnesses are thought to be located in brain and nervous system; therapy is introduced in which doctor and patient talk.

1895   Sigmund Freud publishes *Studies in Hysteria,* in which he proposes that mental illnesses are caused by conflicts buried in the unconscious.

late 1970s Behavior therapy and medications that affect the levels of neurotransmitters in the brain are used in treating anxiety disorders.

1980   PTSD is first described in the *DSM-III.*

1990s   Brain-imaging technology allows researchers to watch the brains of patients with anxiety disorders at work; SSRIs are widely used to treat anxiety disorders.

2013   The *DSM-V* is released. It reorganizes anxiety disorders and puts OCD and PTSD into their own sections.

CHAPTER NOTES

Chapter 1. Interfering With Life

1. "David's Journey," *48 Hours*, CBS, January 4, 2001, http://www.cbsnews.com/news/davids-journey-31-01-2002/.

2. John H. Greist, James W. Jefferson, and Isaac M. Marks, *Anxiety and Its Treatment: Help Is Available* (Washington, D.C.: American Psychiatric Press, 1986), 55.

3. Christine Gorman, "The Science of Anxiety: Why Do We Worry Ourselves Sick? Because the Brain Is Hardwired for Fear, and Sometimes It Short-Circuits," *Time*, June 10, 2002, 46, http://content.time.com/time/magazine/article/0,9171,1002605,00.html.

4. Ibid.

5. Edward M. Hallowell, *Worry: Controlling It and Using It Wisely* (New York: Pantheon Books, 1997), 38.

6. Ibid., 58.

7. Ibid.

8. NIH Publication No. 99–4504.

9. *As Good As It Gets,* IMDB, 1997, http://www.imdb.com/title/tt0119822/.

10. Gorman, 46–54.

Chapter 2. Anxiety Disorders in History

1. Ian Osborn, *Tormenting Thoughts and Secret Rituals: The Hidden Epidemic of Obsessive-Compulsive Disorder* (New York: Dell, 2013) 222–223.

2. Erwin H. Ackerknecht, *A Short History of Psychiatry*, trans. Sula Wolff (New York: Hafner Publishing Co., 1968), 10.

3. Osborn, 224–225.

4. Ibid., 211.

5. Ibid., 212.

6. Ibid., 213.

7. Ibid.

8. Judith Rapoport, *The Boy Who Couldn't Stop Washing: The Experience and Treatment of Obsessive-Compulsive Disorder* (New York: E.P. Penguin, 1991), 12.

9. Tamar E. Chansky, *Freeing Your Child from Obsessive-Compulsive Disorder: A Powerful, Practical Program for Parents of Children and Adolescents* (New York: Random House, 2011), 27.

10. Ronald M. Doctor and Ada P. Kahn, *The Encyclopedia of Phobias, Fears, and Anxieties* (New York: Facts On File, 2008), 392.

11. Ibid.

12. Robert Burton, *The Anatomy of Melancholy* (New York: New York Review Books, 2001), 368.

13. Robert Burton, as quoted in John Marshall, *Social Phobia: From Shyness to Stage Fright* (New York: Basic Books, 1994), 39.

14. John H. Greist, James W. Jefferson, and Isaac M. Marks, *Anxiety and Its Treatment: Help Is Available* (Washington, D.C.: American Psychiatric Press, 1986) 120.

15. Jonathan Shay, *Achilles in Vietnam: Combat Trauma and the Undoing of Character* (New York: Atheneum, 2010).

16. American Psychiatric Association, *Diagnostic and Statistical Manual of Mental Disorders*, 5th ed. (Washington, D.C.: American Psychiatric Press, 2013) and American Psychiatric Association, "Highlights of Changes from DSM-IV-TR to DSM-V," accessed March 24, 2015, http://www.dsm5.org/Documents/changes%20from%20dsm-iv-tr%20to%20dsm-5.pdf.

17. David Grady and Richard A. Kulka et al., *Trauma and the Vietnam War Generation: Report of Findings from the National Vietnam Veterans Readjustment Study* (New York: Routledge, 2014), 285.

18. Shay, 165–166.

19. William Shakespeare, *Henry IV, Part I*, act 2, sc. 3, lines 37–64.

20. Richard Gabriel, *No More Heroes* (New York: Hill and Wang, 1987), 4.

Chapter 3. What Is OCD?

1. Judith L. Rapoport, *The Boy Who Couldn't Stop Washing: The Experience and Treatment of Obsessive-Compulsive Disorder* (New York: E P. Dutton, 1991), 21–22.

2. Ibid.

3. American Psychiatric Association, *Diagnostic and Statistical Manual of Mental Disorders*, 5th ed. (Washington, D.C.: American Psychiatric Press, 2013) and American Psychiatric Association, "Highlights of Changes from DSM-IV-TR to DSM-V," accessed March 24, 2015, http://www.dsm5.org/Documents/changes%20from%20dsm-iv-tr%20to%20dsm-5.pdf.

4. Ibid.

5. Ian Osborn, *Tormenting Thoughts and Secret Rituals: The Hidden Epidemic of Obsessive-Compulsive Disorder* (New York: Dell, 2013), 33.

6. American Psychiatric Association.

7. Ibid.

8. Rapoport, 6.

9. Tamar E. Chansky, *Freeing Your Child from Obsessive-Compulsive Disorder: A Powerful, Practical Program for Parents of Children and Adolescents* (New York: Random House, 2011), 34.

10. Dr. Daniel Gellar, as cited in Chansky, *Freeing Your Child*, 33.

11. Dr. Gregory Hanna, as cited in Chansky, *Freeing Your Child*, 34.

12. Osborn, 188.

13. Ibid., 190.

14. Chansky, 31.

15. Osborn, 185.

16. Ibid., 68, 88.

Chapter 4. What Are Phobias?

1. John R. Marshall, *Social Phobia: From Shyness to Stage Fright* (New York: Basic Books, 1994), 70–71.

2. American Psychiatric Association, *Diagnostic and Statistical Manual of Mental Disorders*, 5th ed. (Washington, D.C.: American Psychiatric Press, 2013) and American Psychiatric Association, "Highlights of Changes from DSM-IV-TR to DSM-V," accessed March 24, 2015, http://www.dsm5.org/Documents/changes%20from%20dsm-iv-tr%20to%20dsm-5.pdf.

3. Marshall, 93.

4. American Psychiatric Association.

5. National Institute of Mental Health, "Social Phobia (Social Anxiety Disorder): Always Embarrassed," 2013, http://www.nimh.nih.gov/health/publications/social-phobia-social-anxiety-disorder-always-embarrassed/index.shtml.

6. American Psychiatric Association.

7. Marshall, 46.

8. NIMH, "Social Phobia (Social Anxiety Disorder): Always Embarrassed."

9. Lesley Jane Seymour, "Fear of Almost Everything," *Mademoiselle*, September 1993, 254.

10. NIMH, "Social Phobia (Social Anxiety Disorder): Always Embarrassed."

11. American Psychiatric Association.

12. National Institute of Mental Health, "Specific Phobias," accessed February 12, 2015, http://www.nimh.nih.gov/health/topics/anxiety-disorders/specific-phobias.shtml.

13. Ibid.

14. Ibid.

Chapter 5. Panic Attacks and Panic Disorder

1. Martin E. P. Seligman, *What You Can Change and What You Can't: The Complete Guide to Successful Self-Improvement* (New York: Vintage, 2011), 61.

2. American Psychiatric Association, *Diagnostic and Statistical Manual of Mental Disorders*, 5th ed. (Washington, D.C.: American Psychiatric Press, 2013) and American Psychiatric Association, "Highlights of Changes from DSM-IV-TR to DSM-V," accessed March 24, 2015, http://www.dsm5.org/Documents/changes%20from%20dsm-iv-tr%20to%20dsm-5.pdf.

3. Alan Goldstein and Barry Stainback, *Overcoming Agoraphobia: Conquering Fear of the Outside World* (New York: Viking, 1987), 148.

4. M. M. Weissman, as cited in William D. Kernodle, *Panic Disorder: What You Do Not Know May Be Dangerous to Your Health* (Richmond, Va.: William Byrd Press, 1993), 20.

5. M. M. Weissman. "Family genetic studies of panic disorder," *Journal of Psychiatric Research* 27 (1993): 69-78.

6. National Institute of Mental Health, "Panic Disorder: When Fear Overwhelms," accessed April 10, 2015, http://www.nimh.nih.gov/health/publications/panic-disorder-when-fear-overwhelms/index.shtml.

7. Ibid.

8. American Psychiatric Association.

9. National Institute of Mental Health.

Chapter 6. What Is PTSD?

1. Jonathan Shay, *Achilles in Vietnam: Combat Trauma and the Undoing of Character* (New York: Atheneum, 2010), iv.

2. Ibid., xvii.

3. Ibid., 116–117.

4. American Psychiatric Association, *Diagnostic and Statistical Manual of Mental Disorders*, 5th ed. (Washington, D.C.: American Psychiatric Press, 2013) and American Psychiatric Association, "Highlights of Changes from DSM-IV-TR to DSM-V," accessed March 24, 2015, http://www.dsm5.org/Documents/changes%20from%20dsm-iv-tr%20to%20dsm-5.pdf

5. Ibid., 463.

6. NIMH, "Post-Traumatic Stress Disorder (PTSD)," accessed February 12, 2015, http://www.nimh.nih.gov/health/publications/post-traumatic-stress-disorder-ptsd/index.shtml.

7. Erica Goode, "Stress From Attacks Will Chase Some into the Depths of Their Minds, and Stay," *The New York Times*, September 18, 2001, B 1, 11. http://www.nytimes.com/2001/09/18/us/nation-challenged-psychological-trauma-stress-will-chase-some-into-depths-their.html.

8. Ibid., B 11.

Chapter 7. Generalized Anxiety Disorder

1. Edward M. Hallowell, *Worry: Controlling It and Using It Wisely* (New York: Pantheon Books, 1997), 184.

2. Ibid., xiv.

3. American Psychiatric Association, *Diagnostic and Statistical Manual of Mental Disorders*, 5th ed. (Washington, D.C.: American Psychiatric Press, 2013) and American Psychiatric Association, "Highlights of Changes from DSM-IV-TR to DSM-V," accessed March 24, 2015, http://www.dsm5.org/Documents/changes%20from%20dsm-iv-tr%20to%20dsm-5.pdf.

4. "Mental Health: A Report of the Surgeon General: Other Mental Disorders in Children and Adolescents," chapter 3, section 6, accessed February 12, 2015, http://profiles.nlm.nih.gov/ps/retrieve/ResourceMetadata/NNBBHS.

5. Donald W. Goodwin, *Anxiety* (New York: Oxford University Press, 1986), 102–103.

6. National Institute of Mental Health, "Generalized Anxiety Disorder (GAD)," accessed February 12, 2015, http://www.nimh.nih.gov/health/topics/generalized-anxiety-disorder-gad/index.shtml.

7. Ibid.

8. James Morrison, *DSM-5 Made Easy: The Clinician's Guide to Diagnosis* (New York: Guilford Press, 2014).

9. Ibid., 284–285.

Chapter 8. Treating Anxiety

1. Andrew Solomon, *The Noonday Demon: An Atlas of Depression* (New York: Scribner, 2014), 112.

2. Ibid., 114–118.

3. Tamar E. Chansky, *Freeing Your Child from Obsessive-Compulsive Disorder: A Powerful, Practical Program for Parents of Children and Adolescents* (New York: Random House, 2011), 108.

4. Ibid., 6.

5. Ibid., 57.

6. Ian Osborn, *Tormenting Thoughts and Secret Rituals: The Hidden Epidemic of Obsessive-Compulsive Disorder* (New York: Dell, 2013), 70.

7. Ibid., 68.

8. Osborn, 73–75.

9. Ibid., 69.

10. John R. Marshall, *Social Phobia: From Shyness to Stage Fright* (New York: Basic Books, 1994), 180.

11. Ibid.

12. Edward M. Hallowell, *Worry: Controlling It and Using It Wisely* (New York: Pantheon Books, 1997), 172.

13. Ibid., 175.

14. K. Meyerbröker, P.M. Emmelkamp. "Virtual reality exposure therapy in anxiety disorders: a systematic review of process-and-outcome studies," *Depression and Anxiety* (October 27, 2010): 933-44.

15. Ibid.

16. Edmund Jacobson, as cited in Edmund J. Bourne, *The Anxiety and Phobia Workbook, 6th ed.* (Oakland, Calif.: New Harbinger Publications, 2015), 39.

17. Bourne, 68

18. Raymond B. Flannery Jr., *Post-Traumatic Stress Disorder: The Victim's Guide to Healing and Recovery* (Brooklyn, N.Y.: American Mental Health Foundation Books, 2015), 208.

Chapter 9. Anxiety, Society, and Research

1. National Institute of Mental Health, "Anxiety Disorders," accessed February 12, 2015, http://www.nimh.nih.gov/health/publications/anxiety-disorders/index.shtml.

2. Anxiety and Depression Association of America, "Facts and Statistics," accessed February 12, 2015, http://www.adaa.org/about-adaa/press-room/facts-statistics.

3. Ibid.

4. National Institute of Mental Health; Anxiety and Depression Association of America.

5. American Psychiatric Association, *Diagnostic and Statistical Manual of Mental Disorders*, 5th ed. (Washington, D.C.: American Psychiatric Press, 2013) and American Psychiatric Association, "Highlights of Changes from DSM-IV-TR to DSM-V," accessed March 24, 2015, http://www.dsm5.org/Documents/changes%20from%20dsm-iv-tr%20to%20dsm-5.pdf.

6. Ibid., 452.

7. Marcelo Queiroz Hoexter, Fabio Luis de Souza Duran, Carina Chaubet D'Alcante, Darin Dean Dougherty, Roseli Gedanke Shavitt et al., "Gray Matter Volumes in Obsessive-Compulsive Disorder Before and After Fluoxetine or Cognitive-Behavior Therapy: A Randomized Clinical Trial," *Neuropsychopharmacology* 37 (2012): 734–745.

8. Ibid.

9. K. Zimmermann et. al., "Analysis of gastrin-releasing peptide gene and gastrin-releasing peptide receptor gene in patients with agoraphobia." *Psychiatric Genetics* 5 (2014): 232–233.

10. M.M. Weissman. "Family genetic studies of panic disorder," *Journal of Psychiatric Research* 27(1993): 69–78.

11. Anxiety and Depression Association of America.

GLOSSARY

agoraphobia—An anxiety disorder characterized by terror of crowded places, open spaces, or being away from home. Panic attacks are often a part of agoraphobia.

antidepressants—Medications of several types that are used to treat depression and anxiety disorders.

anxiety disorder—A mental disorder with severe anxiety that seriously interferes with one's life. Some types are obsessive-compulsive disorder, phobias, panic disorder and agoraphobia, post-traumatic stress disorder, and generalized anxiety disorder.

anxiety disorder resulting from a general medical condition—An anxiety disorder characterized by severe symptoms of anxiety that result from a medical condition. The anxiety is the physiological result of the illness, not the psychological result of the illness.

cognitive-behavioral therapy (CBT)—Talk therapy that focuses on changing patterns of thought and behaviors that add to psychological problems. CBT is usually shorter in length than traditional psychotherapy.

desensitization—A type of exposure therapy in which the patient is exposed to the feared object or situation in gradually increasing amounts.

exposure therapy—The general term for the types of behavior therapy in which the patient faces the thing he or she fears.

flooding—Exposure therapy in which, with the therapist's support, the patient is immersed in the feared situation. The belief is that if the patient sticks it out, the extreme terror will diminish and be less next time.

generalized anxiety disorder (GAD)—The condition in which the patient worries excessively about a number of different things.

genetics—The scientific study of how genes control the characteristics of plants and animals.

hallucination—An image, a sound, or a smell that seems real but does not really exist and that is usually caused by mental illness or the effect of a drug.

neurotransmitters—Chemical substances that transmit impulses between the spaces between nerves.

obsessive-compulsive disorder (OCD)—An anxiety disorder characterized by obsessions (unwanted, recurring thoughts) and compulsions (repetitive behaviors).

panic attack—A period of extreme terror that builds to a climax. It is accompanied by physical symptoms such as racing heart, dizziness, shortness of breath, and sweating.

panic disorder (PD)—A disorder characterized by expected panic attacks that recur. The person with PD has serious worries about having more attacks.

phobia—An anxiety disorder that is characterized by persistent fears of objects or situations that pose no real threat. The main types of phobias are specific phobia and social phobia.

post-traumatic stress disorder (PTSD)—An anxiety disorder that sometimes follows an extremely traumatic experience, such as combat or an earthquake. The person relives the trauma, is overly alert to new danger, and is not able to experience normal human closeness.

predisposition—Something that causes someone to be more likely to be affected by a particular condition.

specific phobia—A phobia that involves terror of an object or situation.

substance-induced anxiety disorder—An anxiety disorder in which the person experiences extreme anxiety symptoms as a result of intoxication with or withdrawal from certain substances. Alcohol, street drugs, inhalants, and poisons are examples of substances.

symptom—A change in the body or mind that indicates a disease.

FOR MORE INFORMATION

American Psychiatric Association (APA)

psych.org

Promotes research, education, and care for individuals with mental disorders and their families.

Anxiety and Depression Association of America

adaa.org

Supports those with anxiety, depression, OCD, PTSD, and related disorders through education and research.

International OCD Foundation

iocdf.org

Helps individuals with OCD live full and productive lives by increasing access to effective treatment and ending the stigma of mental illness issues.

National Alliance on Mental Illness (NAMI)

nami.org

Offers education programs about mental illness and provides support and referrals.

National Center for PTSD

ptsd.va.gov

Dedicated to research and education on trauma and PTSD.

National Institute of Mental Health

nimh.nih.gov

Dedicated to the prevention, recovery, and cure of mental illnesses including anxiety disorders.

Social Anxiety Association

socialphobia.org

Encourages public awareness of social anxiety, facilitates the use of therapeutic groups, and serves as a resource for all matters related to social anxiety.

FURTHER READING

Brinkerhoff, Shirley. *Obsessive-Compulsive Disorder.* Broomall, Pa.: Mason Crest, 2013.

Chong, Elaine S. *Phobias.* New York: Rosen, 2012.

Collins-Donnelly, Kate. *Starving the Anxiety Gremlin: A Cognitive Behavioural Therapy Workbook on Anxiety Management for Young People.* Philadelphia: Jessica Kingsley, 2013.

Hand, Carol. *Living with Anxiety Disorders.* Edina, Minn.: ABDO, 2014.

Hyman, Bruce M., and Chery Pedrick. *Anxiety Disorders.* Minneapolis: Twenty-First Century Books, 2012.

Latta, Sara. *Scared Stiff: Everything You Need to Know About 50 Famous Phobias.* San Francisco: Zest, 2013.

INDEX

A

acrophobia, 43
adrenaline, 14, 60
agoraphobia, 22–24, 43, 51, 53, 79
amygdala, 14, 60, 89
antianxiety medication, 44, 47, 54,
    64–66, 73, 74, 93
antidepressants, 44, 47, 66, 70–72,
    92
anxiety, benefits of, 12
anxiety-related disorders
    age of onset, 87
    co-occurring conditions, 85–86
    cultural differences, 88
    economic costs of, 87
    fear vs., 11
    history, 17–19
    overview, 6–7
    prevalence, 86
    public awareness of, 14–16
    research on, 89–91
arachnophobia, 43

B

benzodiazepines, 73, 74
beta-blockers, 44
blasphemy, 20, 33
bogeyphobia, 43
brain imaging, 89
brain responses, 12–14
breathing exercise, 81–82
Burton, Robert, 22–24

C

cerebral cortex, 12
Chansky, Tamar, 74
claustrophobia, 43

Climacus, John, 20
cognitive-behavioral therapy
    (CBT)
    GAD, 66
    OCD, 20, 74–75
    overview, 7, 16, 70
    panic attacks, phobias, 47, 54–55,
        77–80
    PTSD, 62, 80–81
    social phobia, 42–44, 75–77
cortisol, 60–62

D

depression, 86
desensitization, 77–79
Diagnostic and Statistical Manual
    of Mental Disorders, 24, 29
diary therapy, 75

E

exposure therapy, 24, 77–79
exposure with response prevention,
    36–37

F

family therapy, 83–84
fight or flight response, 12–14, 50
filth, contamination, 33, 75
flooding, 20–22, 79
Freud, Sigmund, 18, 22, 24

G

generalized anxiety disorder
    (GAD)
    age of onset, 87

causes, onset, treatment, 64–66
diagnosis, 63–64, 69
gender differences, 91
overview, 11, 63
prevalence, 86
genetic mapping, 91

H
habituation, 74–75
Hallowell, Edward, 77–79
hippocampus, 89
Hippocrates, 17, 22
hoarding, 33, 34
hormones, 14, 60–62

K
Khanna, Sumant, 36

L
lactic acid, 53
learned helplessness, 42
lifestyle changes, 93

M
MAOIs (monoamine oxidase
  inhibitors), 72
Marshall, John, 75–77
muscle relaxation, 82

N
neurotransmitters, 36, 71, 72
Nicholson, Jack, 16

O
obsessive-compulsive disorder
  (OCD)
  age of onset, 87
  brain imaging, 89
  causes, 22, 32–36

compulsions, 8–9, 30–32, 34
diagnosis, 30, 32
gender differences, 91
history, 20–22
impacts on life, 8–9, 28–30
obsessions, 33, 74–75
overview, 7–9
prevalence, 86
public awareness of, 16
symptoms, signs, 30–32, 94
treatments, 36–37
twin studies, 32–35
Olivier, Laurence, 44
Osborn, Ian, 37

P
panic attacks, panic disorder
  age of onset, 87
  causes, 50
  defined, 11, 50
  gender differences, 91
  onset, 53
  prevalence, 86
  social phobia vs., 40
  symptoms, signs, 48–50, 54
  treatment, 54–55
  twins studies, 53
performance anxiety, 44
phalacrophobia, 43
phobias
  as adaptive response, 44
  causes, treatment, 47
  defined, 11
  historical descriptions, 22–24
  list of, 43
  onset, 47
  prevalence, 86
  social, 24, 38–44, 86, 87, 91
  specific, 44–46, 79, 91
  symptoms, signs, 38–39
  treatment, 24
post-traumatic stress disorder
  (PTSD)
  age of onset, 87

brain imaging, 89
causes, 27
history, 24–26
onset, 59–62
overview, 7, 11, 59
prevalence, 86
public awareness of, 16
symptoms, signs, 26–27, 56–58, 93
traumas, 27, 58–60, 62, 93
treatment, 62
prescriptions, obtaining, 73–74
psychoanalysis, 18, 20, 24

R
Rapoport, Judith, 32
relaxation techniques, 80–82

S
self-diagnosis, 69
Shakespeare, William, 22
Shay, Jonathan, 56–57
shyness, 40–42
social modeling, 42
social phobia
  as adaptive response, 40–42
  age of onset, 87
  causes, treatment, 42–44
  common, 39
  diagnosis, 40
  gender differences, 91
  onset, 42
  prevalence, 86
  symptoms, signs, 24, 38–40
SSRIs (selective serotonin reuptake inhibitors), 71, 72
Streptococcus, 36
substance abuse, 85
substance-induced anxiety, 67–69

T
TCAs (tricyclic antidepressants), 72
thyroid gland, overactive, 66–67

V
Vietnam War, 24, 26, 56
virtual reality exposure, 79–81

W
Weissman, M. M., 53
White, E. B., 64

Y
Yehuda, Rachel, 60–62